Language, Ethnicity and the State

Volume 1

Also by Camille C. O'Reilly

THE IRISH LANGUAGE IN NORTHERN IRELAND: The Politics of Culture and Identity

LANGUAGE, ETHNICITY AND THE STATE
Volume 2: Minority Languages in Eastern Europe Post-1989 (*editor*)

Language, Ethnicity and the State

Volume 1: Minority Languages in the European Union

Edited by

Camille C. O'Reilly
Lecturer in Social Anthropology
Richmond College
The American International University
London

First published 2001 by
PALGRAVE
Houndmills, Basingstoke, Hampshire RG21 6XS and
175 Fifth Avenue, New York, N. Y. 10010
Companies and representatives throughout the world

PALGRAVE is the new global academic imprint of
St. Martin's Press LLC Scholarly and Reference Division and
Palgrave Publishers Ltd (formerly Macmillan Press Ltd).

ISBN 0–333–92925–X

This book is printed on paper suitable for recycling and
made from fully managed and sustained forest sources.

A catalogue record for this book is available
from the British Library.

Library of Congress Cataloging-in-Publication Data
Language, ethnicity and the state / edited by Camille C. O'Reilly.
    p. cm.
    Includes bibliographical references and index.
    Contents: v. 1. Minority languages in the European Union –
    – v. 2. Minority languages in Eastern Europe post -1989.
    ISBN 0–333–92925–X (vol. 1) — ISBN 0–333–92924–1 (vol. 2)
    1. Linguistic minorities—Europe. 2. Ethnic identity—Europe.
    3. Language policy—Europe. 4. Language planning—Europe.
    5. Europe—Politics and government—1989– I. O'Reilly, Camille.

    P119.32.E85 L28 2001
    306.44'94—dc21

                                             2001021751

10   9   8   7   6   5   4   3   2
10   09   08   07   06   05   04   03   02

Printed and bound in Great Britain by
Antony Rowe Ltd, Chippenham, Wiltshire

Contents

Acknowledgements

I would like to thank Jane Friederichs, Alex Seago, Laura Lengel and Joe Ruane for their support and encouragement during the writing and preparation of this book. Special thanks also to Sharon Foley for reading and commenting on the Introduction, and to Patrizia Fregosi, Peter Kennealy and the librarians at the European University Institute Library in Florence, Italy, for all their help during the time I spent there in June 1999. Thanks also to my family and friends for their love and understanding.

Notes on the Contributors

Tom Cheesman is a lecturer in German at the University of Wales, Swansea. His major publications include *The Shocking Ballad Picture Show: German Popular Literature and Cultural History* (1994) and *Ballads into Books* (co-editor, 1997). He has also written a number of essays, including those on popular ballads, monstrosities, Goethe, Werner Herzog and hip hop. Cheesman is currently working on an ESRC-funded interdisciplinary project on diaspora literary cultures.

Susan DiGiacomo is currently a visiting assistant professor in the Department of Sociology and Anthropology, Middlebury College and an adjunct professor in the Department of Anthropology at the University of Massachussetts, Amherst. She began to study Catalan nationalist discourse, political identity formation and language ideology in 1977. Her publications include book chapters and journal articles on language politics and the Catalan experience of Spain's democratic transition; language ideological debates in the context of the 1992 Olympic Games in Barcelona; and the tension between images of the rural and the urban in both historical and contemporary Catalan political discourse. DiGiacomo's interests in ideology, discourse and power in complex societies extend into other domains as well: cancer treatment and epidemiology, political violence and changing labour conditions in academic employment.

Alexandra Jaffe is associate professor of Anthropology at the University of Southern Mississippi. Her research on Corsica has focused on the influence of dominant language ideologies on everyday practices, minority language revitalization strategies and popular responses to Corsican language planning. Her book on Corsica, *Ideologies in Action: Language Politics on Corsica*, was published in 1999. Jaffe has also published on the social meanings of greeting cards and (with Shana Walton) on the implications of orthographic choice for stigmatized language varieties.

Camille C. O'Reilly is lecturer in Social Anthropology at Richmond, the American International University in London. She is the author of a number of articles on nationalism and the Irish language revival; gender, nationalism and the Irish language; the Irish language as symbol; the Irish language movement and the peace process in Northern Ireland; the politics of culture in Northern Ireland, and (with Gordon McCoy) the Ulster-Scots language. She is also the author of *The Irish Language in Northern Ireland: the Politics of Culture and Identity* (1999). O'Reilly is currently researching long-haul independent travel and 'backpacker' tourism.

Dónall Ó Riagáin has a long career in promoting lesser used languages and cultures. An economist by training, he worked in industry and the savings and credit cooperative movement before becoming professionally involved in the Irish language movement. He has worked with the Irish language and cultural organization *Gael-Linn*, and served on the Advisory Planning Committee of *Bord na Gaeilge*, the Republic of Ireland's language promotion agency. He was one of the founders of the European Bureau for Lesser Used Languages, and was the organization's first president from 1982 to 1984, and then its Secretary-General until 1998. He has been a member of the Advisory Council of the European Centre for Minority Issues since 1999.

Jaro Stacul is a post-doctoral research associate at the Department of Social Anthropology, University of Cambridge, and editor of the journal *Cambridge Anthropology*. His current research is on issues of national and regional identity in Europe in the context of globalization, and on the cultural construction of the past. His main interests are the ways in which political ideologies accommodate themselves to local-level discourses, and especially the capacity of social actors to interpret political symbols emanating from national, regional and other centres. Stacul's publications include the chapter 'The Appropriation of Tradition: the Shifting Meaning of Hunting in the Italian Alps', in T. Dekker, J. Helsloot, C. Wijers (eds) *Roots and Rituals: Managing Ethnicity* (forthcoming).

Lenora Timm is professor and chair of Linguistics at University of California, Davis. Her research and teaching interests include general linguistics, sociolinguistics, minority languages, bilingualism, Breton language and culture, language and gender, women's studies and ecofeminism. Timm is the author of numerous scholarly articles, reviews and a book on a major Breton poet: *A Modern Breton Political Poet – Anjela Duval*. More recently, she is a contributor, as translator, of Breton poetry appearing in the anthology *Writing the Wind: a Celtic Resurgence*, ed. Thomas Rain Crowe (1997).

1
Introduction: Minority Languages, Ethnicity and the State in the European Union[1]

Camille C. O'Reilly

The political and social upheaval of the 1990s have had significant implications for the minority languages of Western Europe, sometimes heartening in terms of the survival and prosperity of minority languages, but more often deeply disturbing. It is difficult to see the ethnic revivals within the European Union[2] in quite the same light after events that have occurred in Eastern Europe throughout the last decade.[3] Still, developments within the EU during the 1990s, from the perspective of stateless and minority ethnic groups, have been largely positive.

This book has two primary aims. The first is to bring together a selection of sociological/ethnographically oriented work, drawn from a number of different disciplines, to allow the reader to make comparisons between developments in different ethno-linguistic revival movements within the EU. The second, closely related, goal is to explore the impact of EU policy and discourse on individual movements within states, and on the orientation of Western Europe as a whole towards linguistic heterogeneity and cultural diversity.

By the close of the tumultuous and often violent twentieth century, it was clear that ethnicity and nationalism had become the primary political idioms, displacing class and overshadowing other issues and other possible modes of political organization. During the last 100 years we have become all too familiar with the destructive potential of ethnic nationalism, and while the politics of ethnicity and identity have been a liberating force in some cases, they have also been used to mask or deny relations of power and ideology which underpin inequality and conflict in much of the world.

With the spread of nationalism as the dominant mode of political organization and the rise of ethnicity as a key means of constructing

1

and expressing group identity, identity politics have become part of a hegemonic discourse and political practice. Just as every human being has a gender identity, we must now all have an ethnic identity as an integral and 'primordial' aspect of our sense of individual self and group membership. A dominant political theme of recent years is that all identities must be respected and understood in their own terms, often leading to extremes of cultural relativism which require acceptance and stifle opposition or dissent. In the politics of ethnicity, culture is paramount as well as virtually untouchable, reified and incorporated into a hegemonic discourse of identity.[4]

The rise of identity politics has been accompanied by a certain conflation of the three concepts culture, ethnicity and nation, with the terms being used almost interchangeably in some contexts, not just in popular usage but in the academic literature as well. It seems prudent, then, to clarify their meanings and briefly to examine the inter-relationships between them. While it is likely that there have always been groups formed on the basis of perceived cultural difference and shared blood or kinship, ethnic affiliation began to take on a new significance in the post-war era. Since its first appearance in the social science literature in the 1950s,[5] the term ethnicity has clearly caught hold of the popular and academic imagination. In the space of just a few years, ethnicity has come to be seen as a key aspect of identity, which, along with gender, sexual identity and social class, is central to the construction and negotiation of status and power in state societies (Alonso 1994, p. 391). In spite of (or perhaps because of) its popularity, its meaning tends to be a bit fuzzy, indicating anything from the essence of an ethnic group, or the sense of belonging to an ethnic group, or that which an ethnic group has that makes it distinct from other ethnic groups (Tonkin *et al.* 1989).

Bringing together key elements of the literature on ethnicity, Hutchinson and Smith suggest that an ethnic group generally exhibits six main features to varying degrees: (1) a common proper name; (2) a myth of common ancestry or fictive kinship; (3) shared historical memories; (4) one or more elements of a common culture, usually including religion, customs or language; (5) a link with a homeland, whether or not the ethnic group still occupies the territory; and (6) a sense of solidarity on the part of at least some of the group (Hutchinson and Smith 1996, pp. 6–7). The degree of incorporation of the group clearly varies between ethnic groups and within the same group over time, as does the extent to which ethnicity is used as a basis for political organization and action.

According to common sense notions of the concept, ethnicity is perceived as a 'natural' part of being human. The existence of particular ethnic groups tends to be projected into the distant past and the significance of ethnic identity for an individual's social standing and status is largely taken for granted. In the academic literature, this perspective is often labelled primordialist, in contrast to instrumentalist and constructivist approaches. Primordialists tend to emphasize depth and 'givenness' of ethnic ties, relating them to ties of 'blood' and kinship, while instrumentalists tend to see ethnicity as a social and political resource that can be used in the competition for wealth, power and status.[6] Constructivists, who may or may not be instrumentalists as well, emphasize the modernity of ethnic groups and highlight how they are constructed through social interaction, in particular political and historical contexts. The three approaches are not necessarily mutually exclusive, and many academics tend to draw on a combination of these in practice. In popular usage, however, the primordialist view dominates, a fact that needs to be taken into account in any attempt to understand the workings of the politics of ethnicity and identity.

It is important to avoid overly reductionist explanations of ethnicity, particularly the implication that it is 'tribal' or in some way tied to our more 'primitive' nature. The rise of ethnicity is not a 'return' to the atavistic, but rather a concept that has been developed and applied in particular ways during the late twentieth century. We get no further in our attempt to understand it by dismissing it as somehow natural or an inevitable feature of humanity. Indeed, such thinking on the part of social scientists and other social commentators can contribute to what Schöpflin refers to as reductionist mobilization, 'the state of affairs where all questions, problems arguments, demands, and so on are interpreted exclusively in ethnonational terms' (Schöpflin 1995, p. 47). When political articulation is reduced to just this one channel, the compromises and deals that normally characterize democratic systems cannot take place. Schöpflin argues that once deep-level cultural issues come to the fore, material concessions or incentives become useless, since issues of cultural identity are difficult to bargain away (Schöpflin 1995).

At the same time, we should also resist the temptation to see ethnicity in overly instrumental terms. Emphasizing that all ethnic identities are constructed in particular historical, social and political circumstances does not mean that 'anything goes' in the formation of ethnic groups and the mobilization of ethnic movements. The cultural features that are chosen to mark boundaries between ethnic groups often have fundamental, persistent and deep meanings for the people concerned, and cannot be brushed aside as mere manipulation to serve the aims of elites. As Smith (1986) has pointed out, aspects of culture and history can be fashioned to support and promote present-day needs, but these constructions take place within and are constrained by existing contexts.[7] It is true that ethnic identity can be politicized; indeed, it can be consciously created for expressly political purposes in some instances (Hanf 1995), but this does not necessarily mean that ethnic identity is shallow or without significance for members of the group in question.

There tends to be a great deal of slippage between the terms culture and ethnicity, again both in popular usage and the academic literature. It could be argued that while any subjectively identifiable group might share a common culture, ethnicity is a conscious awareness of that sharing (Schöpflin 1995, p. 42). Roosens (1995) points out that, in fact, cultural identity may or may not be congruent with ethnic identity. The primary reason why the terms culture and ethnicity are confused stems from the fact that people tend to use only a limited number of emic cultural traits to define themselves ethnically (Roosens 1995, pp. 30–1). It is quite common for people to categorize themselves into two distinct ethnic groups in spite of having, from an outsider's perspective, a great deal of shared culture in common. Ethnic identification is also a narrower form of classification, implying the exclusion of those who are not members of the group. It is entirely possible, on the other hand, to freely acknowledge shared cultural traits across ethnic groups. For example, it is not unusual to speak of a common European culture or specifically European cultural traits, while at the same time acknowledging the ethnic diversity within the region. In addition, culture can change over time, while the ethnic group associated with it is perceived as static and continuous.

Ethnic and linguistic revival movements are sometimes – but not invariably – associated with nationalism and nationalist movements, as the chapters in this volume will attest. In some cases, the association is strong and nationalism is a prominent feature of minority language movements, as with Catalan (DiGiacomo, this volume), Corsican (Jaffe, this volume) and the Irish language in Northern Ireland (O'Reilly, this volume). In others, regional identity is more prominent than either language issues or nationalism (Stacul, this volume), or nationalism plays a more minor or background role (Timm on Brittany; O'Reilly on the Republic of Ireland, this volume). Ethnic and nationalist revival movements can have both constructive and destructive aspects. The politicization of ethnicity has been disastrous in many cases but it also holds creative potential, as evidenced by linguistic aspects of many ethnonationalist movements in Europe as described in this collection. As Miller (1998) points out with reference to Northern Ireland, ethnicity and identity are often erroneously pointed to as the irreducible causes of conflict, rather than products of historical contingencies and social, political and economic processes.[8]

There is a substantial literature on nationalism and the relationship between ethnicity and nationalism, a review of which is beyond the scope of this short introduction.[9] It is possible, however, to highlight a few points that are relevant to the general orientation of this volume, particularly in relation to language and state formation. Once again, it is important to clarify the difference between the terms 'state' and 'nation'. For a working definition of the state we can turn to Hobsbawm, who suggests that the modern model consists of 'a territory, preferably coherent and demarcated by frontier lines from its neighbours, within which *all* citizens without exception come under the exclusive rule of the territorial government and the rules under which it operates', the ideal of which is represented by an ethnically, culturally, and linguistically homogeneous population – the nation (1996, pp. 1065–6, emphasis in original).

Many theorists have pointed out that the nation has become the single, over-arching basis of political community in the modern period. It is common, also, to highlight two aspects of nationalism, the civic and the ethnic. While this volume primarily focuses on the ethnic aspects of nationhood and nationalism, it is worth emphasizing that the power of nationalist ideology derives at least in part from the potent combination of the ideal of popular sovereignty and universal citizenship (the civic element), and the ideal of shared culture as an agent of political legitimization and mark of authenticity (the ethnic element). Although often portrayed as ideal types, the two work in combination in real world situations. As Schöpflin points out, while most nations benefit from an ethnic base, this alone is not sufficient foundation on which to build the political community of a state. Likewise, civic unity has proven too weak on its own to form the basis of the states that have taken shape during the last two centuries. The civic and ethnic elements have developed together, sometimes in competition, sometimes overlapping, in an ongoing process of definition and redefinition that continues to the present day (Schöpflin 1995, pp. 40–1).

On the thorny topic of the modernity of nations, the strong versions of both constructivism and the primordialism sometimes go too far. The mass of evidence suggests that nationalism is indeed a modern ideology that has developed along with the dramatic socio-economic, cultural and political changes wrought by industrialization.[10] In other words, nations, like ethnic groups, are constructed within the constraints of particular historical, social and cultural contexts. It is also fair to say that some nations can draw on relatively deep ethnic roots, while others cannot. As Gellner so eloquently puts it:

> Some nations have navels, some achieve navels, some have navels thrust upon them. Those possessed of genuine ones are probably in a minority, but it matters little. It is the need for navels engendered by modernity that matters. (1997, p. 101)

Although nationalism tends to be portrayed as universal, perennial and wholly self-evident (Gellner 1997, p. 7), it is important that we continue to point out that there is indeed nothing 'natural' about it.

There is little doubt that the dramatic events that took place in Europe during the 1990s have forced us to look at nationalism and ethnic movements in a new light. After the horrors of the second world war, nationalism as a political ideology took on a certain pariah status. With its destructive aspect in the forefront of the popular imagination, the legitimacy of ethnic or national politics seemed to have been seriously undermined. When the ethnic revival took hold in Europe from the 1960s onwards, efforts were made both to limit its potential impact on the one hand, and to interpret it as something other than what it turned out to be, that is, the resurgence of ethnic politics (Schöpflin 1995, p. 38). Schöpflin suggests a variety of factors that might have caused the resurgence:

> dissatisfaction with the increasing remoteness of the state, particularly in its technological-technocratic manifestation as in France and Britain; the renewed self-confidence of greater prosperity; and the narrowing of horizons with the end of empire and the demand for greater democratic control based on the cultural community rather than the state where these latter two did not coincide. (1995, p. 46)

Crucially, the majority of these new ethnic movements have not called the integrity of the state into question; rather, they usually look for increased access to power or a degree of autonomy within existing state structures. While the exceptions to this general statement have in some cases involved significant levels of violence, as in Northern Ireland and the Basque Country, other ethnic movements with a nationalist element or wing have successfully used non-violent means to pursue their goals. This is in sometimes stark contrast to the rise of nationalist movements in Eastern Europe during the 1990s, such as those that split apart Yugoslavia and rocked the Soviet successor states.[11]

It is possible to understand this to some extent with reference to Gellner's division of Europe into four 'zones', roughly corresponding to differences in the relationship between culture and state. Zone one consists of the societies spread out along the Atlantic coast, including the strong dynastic states centred around Lisbon, Madrid, Paris and London. Gellner suggests that a dominant, relatively uniform culture roughly coincided with the state in the post-medieval era, long before the age of nationalism deemed this essential. He argues that although there were smaller cultures within the zone that were not associated with their own states, the most significant cultural differences were to be found between social strata rather than between regions. When nationalism came into existence, no great changes were required. In fact, the only major change to take place in this zone after the advent of nationalism was the creation of the Republic of Ireland (Gellner 1997, pp. 50–1).

Zone two lies immediately to the east and corresponds roughly to the territory of the Holy Roman Empire. Here, according to Gellner, the situation was somewhat more complicated. While a 'high' culture existed in Italy and Germany that might form the basis of nationalism, there was no pre-existing state because of the region's history of political fragmentation. In this zone, unification became a central issue. The outlines of a state structure were sought via the monarchies of Piedmont and Prussia respectively, and a form of nationalism developed which sought to create a unified territory for a 'nation' which in some senses already existed (Gellner 1997, pp. 52–3). In this second zone, nationalism did eventually develop into a particularly virulent form, leaving a legacy of distaste for the ideology which persists into the new century. In zone one, however, it is perhaps less surprising that ethnic and even nationalist movements tend to be more liberal, and more willing to pursue their goals by modifying (rather than overthrowing) existing frameworks. Here it has been easier for activists to emphasize the creative side of nationalism, focusing on its potential for social solidarity while downplaying its potential to foment strife and division.

In spite of the fact that there are no ethnically homogeneous states in Europe whatever the zone,[12] the ideal of the nation-state has persisted into the new century and shows no sign of decline. Even where the goal falls short of establishing an independent state, this ideal forms the basis of ethnic revivalist claims to linguistic and cultural rights and access to power within existing states. How is it that the ideal of the ethnic nation-state persists in the face of such a heterogeneous reality? Part of the answer lies in the nature of the modern state itself.

Alonso points to the tendency in both common sense and academic accounts to reify the state: 'Hegemonic strategies, at once material and symbolic, produce the idea of the state while concretizing the imagined community of the nation ... through the everyday routines, rituals, and policies of the state system' (1994, p. 382). Many state-centred approaches to understanding nationalism, which emphasize the role of the modern state in the formation of ethnic communities and nations, make the mistake of treating the nation with undue concreteness. A partial correction to this tendency might be to look, as Smith has argued, at the other side of the coin as well, focusing on the influence of ethnic origin and culture on state formation (Smith 1996, p. 448).

Another element in an explanation of the persistence of the nationalist ideal of the state can be found within a major philosophical strand of modernism. In the modernist dichotomy between reason, progress and civilization on the one hand, and emotion, tradition and the state of nature on the other, certain languages came to be seen as the vehicles of rational thought while others were deemed 'emotional' or simply inadequate. Those that were believed to have the capacity to promote reason came to be linked to the rational ideal of the modern state, while the others remained 'stateless' and linked to the realm of the traditional. Because the 'stateless' languages tended to be linked to the old order, they were often perceived as a threat to the state and became the subject of neglect or outright hostility. An ideal of homogeneity emerged, with the equation one language equals one state. Language came to be seen as a significant marker of the boundaries between societies and between states, which, according to the emerging nationalist ideal, should be co-terminus. Once this ideal took hold, stateless languages became minority languages, and their speakers became minority ethnic groups. The logic of language, nation and state became circular and, eventually, self-evident – each language group must constitute a nation, each nation should have a state, each state should have just one language.

There is no room for stateless languages in this scenario. Speakers of these languages must either be assimilated into the dominant language and culture, or they might make a claim to nationhood in their own right. It should be clear at this point that the label 'minority' language is a political construct, the product of nationalist ideology and processes of state formation. It has little to do with absolute numbers or demography – numerically there are more speakers of Catalan than Danish, yet the former is generally considered a minority language while the latter is not. To complicate matters, not all minority languages are stateless. Some are extra-territorial state languages, such as German or French, spoken by communities outside the boundaries of their titular states.

The primary issue is relative power – minority languages are 'minor' in relation to what is considered the national language (Haberland 1991, pp. 182–3). Some have suggested that the term minority is oppressive in itself, implying deviance from the norm or inadequacy. The term 'lesser-used language' occasionally appears as an alternative,[13] but this does not really avoid the pitfalls associated with the label 'minority', and it is rather awkward to use. As Haberland points out, *not* using the term minority can also be oppressive, especially when the group in question clearly identifies itself as such. Avoidance of the term can be a means to define a group out of existence, as when Kurds are referred to as 'Mountain Turks' by the Turkish authorities (1991, pp. 180–1). A further distinction is sometimes made between regional and minority languages, with the term 'regional' referring to those languages with a fairly large territory, and 'minority' to those with a small territory, limited development potential, and whose survival appears to be threatened (Tabouret-Keller 1991, p. 49). The problem with this distinction is the difficulty in defining the precise distinguishing characteristics between the two, and its rather simplistic association between number of speakers and relative vitality of a language group.

Minority language groups are very often located on the periphery of states, and are marginalized not just symbolically and politically, but in material terms as well (Alonso 1994, p. 392; Smith 1996; *Euromosaic* 1996). The authors of *Euromosaic*[14] suggest that the categorization of minority language groups as deviations from the norm of state homogeneity is one factor that has actually generated marginality (1996, p. 59). Eriksen (1992) points out that contrary to popular misconception, geographical and economic isolation does not protect minority languages. To the contrary, he cites many examples which indicate that the most isolated language groups are the most under threat – paradoxically never more so than when often well-meaning attempts at economic restructuring and revitalization encroach into their territory. The irony is that speakers of minority languages must learn to deal with the majority culture – including learning to speak the dominant language – in order to assert and protect their rights and identity. Eriksen argues that integration into the modern economic and political order is essential to minority language survival. This conclusion can be elaborated upon with reference to the results of the *Euromosaic* study, which clearly indicates that any economic develop-ment needs to be combined with considerable state support in order for the minority language group to accommodate and benefit from this sort of change. Economic restructuring in the absence of state support can result in the elimination of the minority language (*Euromosaic* 1996, p. 43).

Whether or not this happens successfully depends very much on the relationship between the minority language and the state in relation to three factors: institutionalization, legitimacy and legal status. Institutionalization refers to 'the extent to which a language is institu-tionalized in a variety of contexts so that it is employed without any reflection on the part of the public in general', or what is sometimes referred to as normalization (*Euromosaic* 1996, p. 12; see also DiGiacomo, this chapter). Legitimacy can be linked to legislation or social policies that relate directly to minority languages, but more often it has to do with ideas about appropriateness and expectations – forces that operate primarily on the level of discourse rather than as consciously held beliefs. Legislation alone may help to confer legitimacy on a language, but language use in the sense of institution-alization is not necessarily affected by official policies or laws (*Euromosaic* 1996).

The policy of the state in which a minority language group is located is an obvious and clearly significant factor for the vitality and long-term survival of the language, but not necessarily the most important one. The support of the state can be crucial for language production and reproduction,[15] particularly in terms of resources for education and media. Although the Irish language is in some senses an anomaly in that it is both a 'minority' language and an official language of the Republic of Ireland, its relatively weak position indicates that state support alone is not enough. The demographic size of a language group is another fact which is often considered to be significant in terms of the vitality of a minority language, but again the relationship is not as straightforward as one might assume. Generally speaking, larger language groups are more successful in terms of reproduction, but some of the numerically smaller groups in the *Euromosaic* study are doing just as well as, if not better than, some of the larger groups. As might be expected, the *Euromosaic* study also found a fairly clear correlation between the role of a minority language in the education system and the prestige of that language.

One of the truly significant developments in relation to minority languages in the post-war decades has been the formation and development of the European Union. While it is likely that the individual states that make up the EU will continue to exert a significant influence on minority language groups, the impact of the EU should not be underestimated. The EU has provided both a new forum for minority language groups to voice their demands and concerns and new institutional structures through which to pursue their objectives. It has also allowed for an increased degree of collaboration between minority language groups across state borders. As Coulmas points out, many linguistic minorities are tiny, but taken together they number in the tens of millions (Coulmas 1991, p. 14; Forrest 1998, p. 314).

The EU has come out strongly in support of multilingualism, paradoxically *because of* the strong monolingualism of its member states. It is the great importance that EU member states attach to their national languages which has necessitated the linguistic pluralism of the EU. Whatever the original motivation, the emphasis on linguistic and cultural diversity has provided an opening for minority language groups to make their case. However supportive the EU may seem ideologically, though, there has actually been very little in terms of concrete action in support of minority languages on the part of the Council of Ministers. There are a number of reasons for this. First, there is still little provision for a common cultural or educational policy in the EU, and the issue of cultural integration remains a controversial topic. Because language issues fall into this category, they have received scant attention – all the more so for minority languages, which are particularly likely to stir up conflict within and between member states. Another important reason for the lack of concrete action is the principal of subsidiarity (Article 3b of the EC Treaty), which states that the EU should only undertake those responsibilities of governance that it can solve more effectively than if individual countries tackled the issue at the state level. A member state could argue that they are capable of supporting any minority languages within their borders, and that therefore the EU should not intervene. Perhaps a more straightforward reason is that there is only a limited amount of funding available for linguistic activities, and much of this is spent on the promotion of multilingualism in the official languages of the EU (Forrest 1998, p. 316).

The European Parliament has been both the most sympathetic of the EU institutions and the main impetus for action related to minority languages. It has prepared a series of reports and adopted significant resolutions relating to linguistic and cultural minorities, encouraged the European Commission to take initiatives; it has also used its budgetary powers to create an EU budget line that has funded projects such as the European Bureau for Lesser Used Languages (see Ó Riagáin, this volume) and the *Euromosaic* study. In the conclusion to that study, the authors assert the value of cultural and linguistic diversity not just in cultural terms, but in terms of economic competitiveness and entrepreneurial potential. On this basis, they call for a pro-active policy that addresses the relationship between the economic development of minority language communities and state language planning if the minority languages of the EU are to survive. When and whether such a policy will ever be implemented on either the state or EU level remains to be seen.

In the meantime, the most significant statement on minority language rights continues to be the Council of Europe's Charter on Regional or Minority Languages. In a similar vein to the European Convention on Human Rights, the charter provides an opportunity for states to subscribe to common principles without making this legally binding. Tabouret-Keller (1991) points out that the terms of the charter are drawn up in such a way that individual states have almost total freedom to define and choose which measures to apply in their own territories. The charter is careful to emphasize that it is pursuing a cultural objective rather than a political one, and consequently avoids sticky issues like providing the definition of a minority language or an actual list of minority languages. Three criteria are provided to determine which languages can be considered under the charter: history, space and language classification. The language must be seen as belonging to the European cultural heritage,[16] it must have a territorial base and must be an identifiably separate language. Ultimately, it is up to individual signatory states to decide which, if any, languages within its territory fit the criteria. The aim of the charter is not to set out the rights of linguistic minorities, but rather to protect regional and minority languages through both non-discrimination and promotion (Tabouret-Keller 1991, p. 49).

The contributions to this volume and the existing literature on ethnicity, identity and the state suggest that a significant trend is unfolding in the context of Western Europe, both philosophical and institutional. It is increasingly common, in the context of Europe, to find a discourse of cultural diversity which stands in opposition to the modernist emphasis on homogeneity.[17] The Maastricht Treaty itself, which came into force in 1993, specifically underlines the importance of the diversity of European cultures (Article 128). Language in particular frequently enjoys special treatment in the discourse on diversity. It is now commonplace to highlight the benefits of bilingualism, particularly with reference to the evidence for increased problem-solving skills in bilingual children, a trait seen as essential to a competitive workforce (CEC Report of Activities 1994, p. 12). The authors of *Euromosaic* conclude that:

> Given what is claimed concerning the importance of diversity as one of the advantages which Europe has over competing regions in the world economy, there is an obvious need to be able to exploit that advantage. ... This leads us to a point which cannot be over-emphasised: the need for a programme of action to promote minority language groups as sources of diversity that derives from language and culture ... not for the benefit of the various language groups as a European heritage, but for the economic advantage of the entire Community. (1996, p. 60)

Laitin writes that the counterpressures of globalization and nationalism can be seen most starkly over issues concerning language (1997, p. 280). Many have argued that globalization has contributed to the trend towards increasing homogeneity of people in the West, often citing the spread and dominance of the English language as evidence. On the other hand, there has been a strong trend towards respect for and revitalization of regional identities and minority languages and cultures, seen in the increasing importance of regions in the economic, political and cultural evolution of the EU. Pluralism and 'multiculturalism' have become a point of powerful political and philosophical discussion. There is not the space here to delve into these debates,[18] but it is important to note the significance of this trend for the future of minority languages in Europe. In the absence of an official *lingua franca* for the EU, there has been some speculation that English will end up as the *de facto* common language (Forrest 1998; Laitin 1997; Coulmas 1991). At the same time, as Coulmas points out, the most promising arena in which to pursue the issue of minority language rights within the European Union is within a regional framework (1991, p. 16).

Laitin (1997), for example, argues that a future European state will have multiple cultural identities, more like the model of India in the twentieth century than France from the eighteenth to the twentieth century. The use of Europe by regional actors as a tool to claim rights and autonomy from centralized institutions of the state may well lead to a normalization of multicultural identities which include a sense of Europeanness along with a regional/ethnic and state/national identity. This will be reflected in multilingualism, with a growing trend towards a '2 ± 1' constellation of language ability. Laitin predicts that in the long term, most native speakers of a state language will speak their mother tongue plus English, while most speakers of non-state or minority languages will speak their mother tongue, the state language and English (as is increasingly the case today in regions such as Catalonia).

The stated goal of the European Union in its various incarnations has been economic and political integration. Cultural matters have been a taboo subject, usually resulting in controversy when raised. As Schöpflin argues, however, once the civic elements of European integration were in place 'the ethnic elements were bound to resurface' (1995, p. 44). There was an underlying assumption that once the economic, administrative, and technological structures were in place, nationalism would simply fade into the background and lose its political saliency. Clearly this has not happened. As the EU continues to evolve and expand to the East, linguistic and cultural issues are likely to become more pressing. We appear to be experiencing a shift from the modernist emphasis on homogeneity, assimilation and unitary identities into an increasingly post-modern focus on difference, heterogeneity and hybrid identities (Grillo 1998), a shift which in the long term will have profound implications for European identities and the survival of minority languages. Whatever the direction this takes us in, it seems clear that ethnicity and nationalism will continue to play a part in European politics well into the twenty-first century.

The chapters in this volume are connected by a number of common threads. The first is an exploration of the impact of European Union policy and discourse on specific minority languages, particularly in relation to the increasing emphasis on regions and the recognition of cultural and linguistic minorities. To start the discussion off in Chapter 2,

Ó Riagáin provides us with background information on the history of EU dealings with minority languages, focusing on the growth and development of the European Bureau for Lesser Used Languages since its establishment in 1982. In Chapter 3, Jaffe discusses French language planning ideologies and strategies in relation to Corsican, showing how over the last 30 years Corsican language planners have been heavily influenced, not just by Corsican ethnic nationalism, but also by French language ideology and linguistic policy. She concludes the chapter by exploring the emergence of new discourses on language and identity influenced by the notion of 'Europe'.

In Chapter 4, DiGiacomo focuses on the process of 'normalizing' Catalan, a language that was once discriminated against but is now experiencing a strong revival. Her contribution highlights a point made by Coulmas (1991) more generally – that Catalan nationalists have seized the opportunities provided by the EU for stateless language groups to make themselves heard and make a positive contribution towards a more egalitarian Europe. My own contribution in Chapter 5 shows how EU membership has influenced the discourses of the Irish language revival in the two parts of Ireland, resulting in different conceptions of the relationship between the language and Irish identity.

Following up on the theme of the importance of language to ethnic and national identities, in Chapter 6, Timm explores the question 'How can one be Breton'?, concluding that after decades of decline, the language's contribution to a sense of Breton identity is variable rather than categorical. In Chapter 7, Stacul discusses the impact of the EU on the (re-)establishment of regional identities, in this case in spite of, rather than because of, linguistic differences. Like Timm, Stacul highlights the importance of non-linguistic aspects of identity, such as common history, territory and economic factors. Finally, in Chapter 8, Cheesman challenges the common distinction made between 'new' and 'old' lesser-used languages in the European Union and its member states, questioning the justness of policies that protect autochthonous languages while ignoring the discrimination against the languages of relative newcomers.

The second thread that ties the contributions together is the relative importance of language to identity. Clearly, there are non-linguistic aspects of ethnic identity such as a sense of kinship and territory, which are often considered more salient than language (Haarman 1991, pp. 106–7). The chapters in this volume fit all along the continuum, covering a case where language is of central importance (DiGiacomo on Catalan), a situation where the language is considered important but is seriously threatened (Jaffe on Corsican), cases where the minority language is no longer used by the majority of the population but is still considered symbolically important (O'Reilly on Irish; Timm on Breton), and finally a case where language takes a back seat to other aspects of regional identity (Stacul on the South Tyrol region).

The final, overarching theme of the book is the move away from an ideal of ethnic homogeneity within states towards a model of cultural and linguistic diversity as a resource, as discussed above. This last theme should be considered in relation to trends in Eastern Europe, which are still largely modernist and homogenizing, with serious consequences for the citizens of that part of the world. In both its destructive and creative aspects, it seems clear that ethnicity and nationalism will continue to be significant forces during the course of the century. It is also likely that current trends towards multiple and hybrid identities will be good news for the future survival of minority languages throughout Europe.

Notes

1. This chapter is based on research carried out at the European University Institute Library under the auspices of EUSSIRF, a Large-Scale Facility funded by the Training and Mobility of Researchers program of the European Commission (DG XXII). Sections of this Introduction also appear in slightly altered form in *Language, Ethnicity and the State: Minority Languages in Eastern Europe, Post-1989.*
2. For the sake of simplicity the term 'European Union' will be used inclusively throughout the book to refer to the EU in its various incarnations up to the present day, including the European Coal and Steel Community and the European Community. Older terms, when they appear, indicate a more specific usage.
3. This book is intended to be read in conjunction with its companion volume 2, *Language, Ethnicity and the State: Minority Languages in Eastern Europe, Post-1989.*
4. For a discussion of this process in relation to nationalism, see Richard Handler's *Nationalism and the Politics of Culture in Quebec* (1988).
5. According to Hutchinson and Smith (1996), the term 'ethnicity' first appeared in the 1953 edition of the *Oxford English Dictionary*. It became popular in the social sciences in the 1970s, with Glazer and Moynihan commenting on the newness of the term in their 1975 edited volume *Ethnicity: Theory and Experience.*
6. See Hutchinson and Smith (1996, pp. 7–10) for a brief synopsis of the primordialist and instrumentalist approaches.
7. See also Benda-Beckman and Verkuyten (1995).

8. See especially chapters by Miller and Clayton in that volume (Miller 1998).
9. For an anthropological perspective on these, see Eriksen (1993) and Banks (1996). See also Jenkins (1997).
10. See especially Anderson ([1983] 1991) and Gellner (1983, 1997).
11. See the companion to this volume, vol. 2, *Language, Ethnicity and the State: Minority Languages in Eastern Europe, Post-1989.*
12. The only real exception to this is Iceland.
13. The term 'lesser-used language' appears in the name of the European Bureau for Lesser-Used Languages – see Ó Riagáin in this volume.
14. *Euromosaic: The Production and Reproduction of the Minority Language Groups of the EU* (1996) is the result of a comprehensive study commissioned by the European Commission. According to the report, the objective of the study 'was to ascertain the current situation of the various language groups by reference to their potential for production and reproduction, and the difficulties which they encounter in doing so' (*Euromosaic* 1996, Executive Summary).
15. The *Euromosaic* study defines reproduction as 'the intergenerational transmission of the language', and production as 'the learning of a language by those whose parents did not speak that language' (1996, pp. 5–6).
16. Cheesman (this volume) challenges whether such a distinction can – or should – be made.
17. See discussions in Coulmas (1991), *Euromosaic* (1996) and Burgess (1999).
18. See Taylor (1994) and Grillo (1998) for background to the debates.

Bibliography

Alonso, A.M. 'The Politics of Space, Time and Substance: State Formation, Nationalism, and Ethnicity', *Annual Review of Anthropology*, 23 (1994) 379–405.

Anderson, B. *Imagined Communities: Reflections on the Origin and Spread of Nationalism*, 2nd edn (London: Verso [1983] 1991).

Banks, M. *Ethnicity: Anthropological Constructions* (London: Routledge, 1996).

von Benda-Beckman, K. and Verkuyten, M. 'Introduction: Cultural Identity and Development in Europe', in K. von Benda-Beckman and M. Verkuyten (eds), *Nationalism, Ethnicity and Cultural Identity in Europe* (Utrecht, The Netherlands: ERCOMER, 1995).

Burgess, A. 'Critical Reflections on the Return of National Minority Rights Regulation to East/West European Affairs', in K. Cordell (ed.), *Ethnicity and Democratisation in the New Europe* (London: Routledge, 1999).

Clayton, P. 'Religion, Ethnicity and Colonialism as Explanations of the Northern Ireland Conflict', in D. Miller (ed.), *Rethinking Northern Ireland* (Harlow, Essex: Longman, 1998).

CEC (Commission of the European Communities), *Lesser Used Languages of the European Union: Report of Activities 1989–1993*, COM(94) 602 Final, CB-CO-94-627-EN-C (Luxembourg: Office for Official Publications of the European Communities, 1994).

Coulmas, F. 'European Integration and the Idea of the National Language: Ideological Roots and Economic Consequences', in F. Coulmas (ed.) *A Language Policy for the European Community: Prospects and Quandaries* (New York: Mouton de Gruyter, 1991).

Eriksen, T.H. 'Linguistic Hegemony and Minority Resistance', *Journal of Peace Research*, 29: 3 (1992) 313–32.

Eriksen, T.H. *Ethnicity and Nationalism: Anthropological Perspectives* (London: Pluto Press, 1993).

Euromosaic: The Production and Reproduction of the Minority Language Groups of the EU (Luxembourg: Office for Official Publications of the European Communities, 1996).

Forrest, A. 'The Politics of Language in the European Union', *European Review*, 6: 3 (1998) 299–319.

Gellner, E. *Nations and Nationalism* (Oxford: Blackwell, 1983).

Gellner, E. *Nationalism* (London: Weidenfeld and Nicolson, 1997).

Glazer, N. and Moynihan, D.A. (eds), *Ethnicity: Theory and Experience* (Cambridge, Mass.: Harvard University Press, 1975).

Grillo, R. *Pluralism and the Politics of Difference: State, Culture and Ethnicity in Comparative Perspective* (Oxford: Clarendon Press, 1998).

Haarman, H. 'Language Politics and the New European Identity', in F. Coulmas (ed.) *A Language Policy for the European Community: Prospects and Quandaries* (New York: Mouton de Gruyter, 1991).

Haberland, H. 'Reflections about Minority Languages in the European Community', in F. Coulmas (ed.) *A Language Policy for the European Community: Prospects and Quandaries* (New York: Mouton de Gruyter, 1991).

Handler, R. *Nationalism and the Politics of Culture in Quebec* (Madison, Wisconsin: Wisconsin University Press, 1988).

Hanf, T. 'Ethnurgy: On the Analytical Use and Normative Abuse of the Concept of "Ethnic Identity"', in K. von Benda-Beckman and M. Verkuyten, (eds), *Nationalism, Ethnicity and Cultural Identity in Europe* (Utrecht, The Netherlands: ERCOMER, 1995).

Hobsbawm, E. 'Language, Culture, and National Identity', *Social Research* 63: 4 (1996) 1065–80.

Hutchinson, J. and Smith, A.D. *Ethnicity*, Oxford Readers (Oxford University Press, 1996).

Jenkins, R. *Rethinking Ethnicity: Arguments and Explorations* (London: Sage, 1997).

Laitin, D.D. 'The Cultural Identities of a European State', *Politics and Society*, 25: 3 (1997) 277–302.

Miller, D. 'Colonialism and Academic Representations of the Troubles', in D. Miller (ed.), *Rethinking Northern Ireland* (Harlow, Essex: Longman, 1998).

Roosens, E. 'Ethnicity as a Creation: Some Theoretical Reflections', in K. von Benda-Beckman and M. Verkuyten, (eds), *Nationalism, Ethnicity and Cultural Identity in Europe* (Utrecht, The Netherlands: ERCOMER, 1995).

Schöpflin, G. 'Nationalism and Ethnicity in Europe, East and West', in C.A. Kupchan (ed.) *Nationalism and Nationalities in the New Europe* (Ithaca and London: Cornell University Press, 1995).

Smith, A.D. *The Ethnic Origin of Nations* (Oxford: Blackwell, 1986).

Smith, A.D. 'Culture, Community and Territory: The Politics of Ethnicity and Nationalism', *International Affairs*, 72: 3 (1996) 445–58.

Tabouret-Keller, A. 'Factors of constraints and Freedom in Setting a Language Policy for the European Community: a Sociolinguistic Approach', in F. Coulmas (ed.) *A Language Policy for the European Community: Prospects and Quandaries* (New York: Mouton de Gruyter, 1991).

Taylor, C. 'The Politics of Recognition', in A. Gutman (ed.), *Multiculturalism* (Princeton, New Jersey: Princeton University Press, 1994).

Tonkin, E. MacDonald, M. and Chapman, M. (eds), *History and Ethnicity* (London: Routledge, 1989).

2

Many Tongues but One Voice: a Personal Overview of the Role of the European Bureau for Lesser Used Languages in Promoting Europe's Regional and Minority Languages

Dónall Ó Riagáin

Europe, post world war II, did not offer a friendly environment to minorities, either their languages, their cultures or their political aspirations. The continent had been ravaged, millions were dead and unemployed and the polarization between the liberal democratic world of Western Europe and that of communist Eastern Europe was becoming all too evident.

Memories were still very much alive of how Hitler had used the presence of German minorities outside the Reich as an excuse for interfering in the internal affairs of other states and in some instances (for example, Czechoslovakia) invading them. There was also the impression, in many instances grossly exaggerated, that disgruntled minorities had collaborated with the invading Nazis (for example, in Flanders and in Brittany) and that the best way forward for Western Europe was to keep such groups firmly in check. If the Western powers did not like Stalin or Tito, the two men at least offered an element of stability, something which so many sought.

In 1948, the UN's Universal Declaration of Human Rights was adopted.[1] The Universal Declaration of Human Rights had nothing to say about the rights of linguistic minorities. However, Article 2 of the Declaration does contain an important reference to language:

Article 2.
Everyone is entitled to all the rights and freedoms set out in this Declaration, without distinction of any kind, such as race, colour, sex, language, religion, political or other opinion, national or social origin, property, birth or other status.

Furthermore, no distinction shall be made on the basis of the political, jurisdictional or international status of the country or territory to which a person belongs, whether it be independent, trust, non-self-governing or under any other limitation of sovereignty.

We see here established the principle that language cannot be used as a basis for denying fundamental human rights to any person.

Other UN agencies (for example, the International Labour Organization and UNESCO) developed this concept in various legal instruments and declarations of their own. The International Labour Organization declared in its convention concerning the protection and integration of indigenous and other tribal and semi-tribal populations in independent countries:[2]

Article 23.
1. Children belonging to the populations concerned shall be taught to read and write in their mother tongue or, where this is not practicable, in the language most commonly used by the group to which they belong.
2. Provision shall be made for a progressive transition from the mother tongue or vernacular language to the national language or to one of the official languages of the country.
3. Appropriate measures shall, as far as possible, be taken to preserve the mother tongue or the vernacular language.'

Reductive bilingualism, maybe, but at least a major step forward from total non-recognition!

UNESCO in its Convention against Discrimination in Education[3] stated in Article 5:

1. The state parties to this convention agree that [...]
(c) It is essential to recognise the rights of members of national minorities to carry on their own educational activities, including the maintenance of schools and, depending on the educational policy of each state, the use of the teaching of their own language ...

Winds of change in Europe

Positive developments came even slower at European level. The Council of Ministers of the European Union, or of the European Communities as it was then known, recognized certain defined official and working languages. The EU, however, made no reference to, or provision for, the regional or minority languages spoken by some millions of its citizens. It is interesting to note that in the original European Coal and Steel Community of 1951 it was envisaged that French be the sole working language. (Indeed, the French text is the only authentic, as distinct from original, version of the treaty.) Protests from the Flemings, who feared that the linguistic balance of Belgium could be disturbed, resulted in Dutch, German and Italian being added. English, Danish, Greek, Spanish, Portuguese, Swedish and Finnish joined the list of official languages as the Community expanded. In addition, Irish is a 'treaty' language – there are versions of the treaties and other basic documents in Irish which are co-official with those in the 11 official and working languages. Furthermore, Irish may be used in the European Parliament and in the Court of Justice subject to certain conditions.

The first signs of interest in the future of the Communities' regional and minority languages appeared in the European Parliament in 1979. On 28 September of that year a motion for resolution was tabled by Gaetano Arfé, MEP, and a number of other Socialist members, all of them from either Italy or France, on a Charter of Ethnic Minorities. Less than a month later, a further motion for resolution was tabled by John Hume, MEP,[4] and co-signed by a Socialist deputy from all the member states calling for the drawing up of a 'Bill of Rights of the Regional Languages and Cultures of the Community'. Although at first glance both motions for resolution seemed very similar, there was in fact a very profound underlying difference in approach between them. Whereas the Arfé Motion for Resolution speaks of 'the demands for autonomy, of ethnic and linguistic minorities', the Hume Motion for Resolution side-steps issues such as ethnicity and autonomy and rather refers to 'this diversity' being 'again one of the main sources of the vitality, richness and originality of European civilisation'. In the event, the European Parliament decided to have two different reports drawn up – one on the rights of ethnic minorities and another on the promotion of regional and minority languages. Gaetano Arfé, MEP, a former professor of history in the University of Firenze and a highly respected parliamentarian, was appointed *rapporteur* of the report on languages whereas the Legal Affairs Committee of Parliament appointed a German Christian Democrat, Mr A. Goppel, to prepare the report on European legislation on ethnic groups. Hume expressed the opinion to the author on a number of occasions that an approach based on ethnicity would never meet with success because it would of its nature trigger off a substantial political reaction. He believed, however, that an approach based on language and culture would strike a chord across the political divides and stood a very good chance of being accepted. Hume's assessment of the situation proved to be correct. The Arfé Report and accompanying motion for resolution came before the plenary session of the Parliament in October 1981.[5] The Goppel Report on the other hand never got past committee stage nor did a subsequent attempt to prepare such a motion for resolution, prepared by Graf Stauffenberg, MEP, and later by Siegbert Alber, MEP.

The Arfé Resolution called on the member state governments and on regional and local authorities to enact a number of measures to support and promote regional and minority languages, particularly in the domains of education, mass communication, public life and social affairs. The motion was adopted by a comfortable majority – 80 votes in favour, 18 against and 8 abstentions. The only political block which voted almost solidly against the resolution was the English Tory group. It was interesting that the Irish Fianna Fáil deputies, who were and still are members of the same political group as the French Gaullists, voted in favour of the resolution but persuaded their French colleagues to abstain rather than vote against the resolution. Most of the 80 votes in favour came from the centre left groupings, especially the Socialists.

Realizing the proposed actions contained in the resolution was another matter and Arfé had the Socialist Group organize a colloquy in Brussels in May 1982 to see how best the proposals, now accepted in principle, could be implemented. Among the invitees were interested MEPs, officials of the European Commission and representatives of most of the lesser used language communities. It became clear that those present, especially the representatives of the languages' movements, were convinced that there was a need to establish a body which could speak and act on their behalf at European level. Thus was born the organization now known as the European Bureau for Lesser Used Languages. A small committee was established and the author was chosen as president. For two years the organization survived on voluntary effort but it was clear from the start that this would not be enough.

The Arfé Resolution led to the opening of a small EU budget line to support measures in favour of regional and minority languages. This was first included in the budget of 1982 and amounted to only 100 000 ECU, as the Euro ('€') was then called. By 1997, this figure had grown to '€'4m.

The Commission agreed to give the Bureau a subvention from this line for specific actions: for example, the publishing of a newsletter; the organization of a study visit programme. This in turn enabled the author to approach the Irish government for additional financial backing. This was forthcoming and with it the political support of a state whose own national language was one of the lesser used. This ongoing Irish political and financial support has proven to be invaluable over the years. The Irish grant-in-aid has increased annually but, more importantly, Ireland insisted on the retention of the small EU budget line when some larger states pressed for its abolition. On one occasion an Irish minister went as far as blocking the entire EU budget until the line for lesser used languages, which had just been dropped by the Budget's Council, was reinstated. The bitten had started to bite.

A second resolution on lesser used languages was adopted by the Parliament in 1983.[6] Again, this resolution was prepared by Gaetano Arfé. It did not contain any new or innovative proposals and its main purpose was to keep pressure on the Commission and on the other EU institutions to fully support and implement the measures contained in the original Arfé Resolution.

The next major initiative on behalf of lesser used languages in the European Parliament came in the form of a report and resolution prepared by Willy Kuijpers, MEP, a Fleming from the Volksunie group.[7] The Kuijpers Resolution, for which Bureau representatives lobbied strenuously, was more ambitious and wide-ranging than the original Arfé Resolution. While more or less respecting the division of domains as outlined by Arfé, it went into greater detail on specific actions which might be taken in different areas. Interestingly, it also called on the Council and Commission to continue their support and encouragement for the European Bureau for Lesser Used Languages by ensuring adequate budgetary resources.

The European Parliament Intergroup for minority languages

Another important development was to take place in 1983 with the establishment of the Intergroup for Minority Languages and Cultures.

An intergroup is an informal committee, comprising MEPs from different political groups, who come together either on a regular or occasional basis because of their interest in a common issue – in this case, in the promotion of lesser used languages. The first meeting was convened on 9 February 1983 under the chairmanship of Gaetano Arfé, MEP. The minutes of this meeting record Mr Arfé as having 'explained the purpose of the meeting, which was to bring together those members of parliament who had shown an interest in promoting minority languages and cultures with a view to working together in parliament to promote and monitor community policies in favour of minority languages and regional cultures'. Unlike many other intergroups, the Intergroup for Minority Languages and Cultures has continued to flourish and over the past 16 years has done sterling work to ensure the development of an EU policy in respect of the Community's linguistic heritage. While the minutes of the first meeting show that, with three exceptions, all of those present were either Socialist or Communist members, the membership of the Intergroup quickly spread to practically all political groups. Such was the respect in which Gaetano Arfé was held that he continued to remain president of the Intergroup until leaving the European Parliament at the time of the 1984 European elections. Since then the presidency has rotated, normally on a six-monthly basis, between one political group and another.

The Killilea Resolution

In 1990, John Hume tabled a motion for a resolution calling for another report on lesser used languages. This time the *rapporteur* chosen was Mark Killilea, MEP. Killilea was an Irish Fianna Fáil deputy and a member of the Union for Europe group whose other members were mostly French Gaullists and Italian members of *Forsa Italia*.

Again, the pivitol role of the Bureau became evident during the preparatory stage of the Killilea Report and Motion for Resolution. Mr Killilea consulted on an ongoing basis with the Bureau and a special researcher, based in the Bureau's Dublin office, was employed to assist him in the preparation of the report. The report itself differed from the earlier Kuijpers and Arfé Reports in that it focused very much on the European Charter for Regional or Minority Languages which had been accorded the status of an international convention by the Committee of Ministers of the Council of Europe in 1992. The Killilea Resolution was wholehearted in its support for the Charter.[8]

The European Parliament [...]

6. Supports the European Charter for Regional or Minority Languages, accorded the legal form of a European Convention, as an effective yet flexible instrument for the protection and promotion of lesser used languages;

7. Calls on the Member State Governments which have not yet done so as a matter of urgency to sign and their parliaments to ratify the Convention choosing at all times to apply those paragraphs best suited to the needs and aspirations of the linguistic communities in question ...

The Bureau threw its weight wholeheartedly into lobbying for support for the resolution. When the vote was taken there were 321 votes in favour with only one vote against and six abstentions.

This landslide vote in favour of the most ambitious resolution yet to be put to the parliament in favour of lesser used languages is an invaluable yardstick in assessing the success of the Bureau's lobbying work and the shift in public opinion in favour of these languages.

The structure of the European Bureau

The Bureau's basic unit of organization is the Member State Committee (MSC). An MSC should be representative of all lesser used language communities in the member state and, as far as possible, should have representatives of the main governmental agencies working in favour of lesser used languages – be they at national, regional or local level – on it. Major voluntary associations should also be represented. While official agencies are strongly represented on some Member State Committees (for example, in Ireland and Finland) political culture in other countries dictates that official and voluntary organizations do not sit together on the same committee but rather interface constructively in other ways. Each MSC chooses two persons to represent it on the Council of the Bureau and it is these people who constitute the official membership of the Bureau. The Council normally meets two or three times per year and every three years elects a president, two vice-presidents and a board of directors. Normally there are six directors, including the president, and two vice-presidents. On election, the president ceases to represent his MSC and is replaced by another nominee. This is intended to ensure the independence of the president in discharging his duties. Until the present time, the Bureau has had two Catalan presidents (one each from France and Spain), two from Ireland

and one each from Gaelic-speaking Scotland, Brittany, Wales and the Slovene community in Italy.

The Bureau has offices in both Dublin and Brussels. From 1984 until 1992, its sole office was in Dublin but increased funding from the European Commission enabled it to open an information centre in Brussels. In 1999, the Secretariat-General was moved from Dublin to Brussels. For a two-year period (1993 until 1995) the Bureau also had a small education secretariat in Luxembourg. A withdrawal of funding by the European Commission forced the Bureau to close this office.

The Bureau is incorporated in Ireland as a company limited by guar-antee but not having a share capital and as an Association Internationale under Belgian law. An interesting footnote is that the bureau was the first company registered in Ireland to lodge its annual audited accounts in the Companies Office in Euros – and, in addition, they were in Irish!

The Bureau receives approximately 90 per cent of its income in the form of subventions from the European Commission. These are paid, not as a type of general grant-in-aid, but as subventions in respect of specific projects. The remainder of the Bureau's funding comes from a variety of sources but mostly from the Department for Arts, Heritage, the Gaeltacht and Islands of the Irish Government which provides the Bureau with a subvention of over '€'50 000 per annum. Smaller sub-ventions are received annually from the governments of Luxembourg, the Province of Friesland and the Deutschesprachige Gemeinschaft Belgiens, the German-speaking community in Belgium. It is also worth noting that the Bureau receives considerably indirect support from regional and local governments throughout Europe. The most notable ongoing example of this is the provision of rent-free office accommo-dation in the heart of Brussels by the Communauté française in Belgium. Various meetings of the Bureau's council, board of directors, working groups and so on, have been hosted over the years by differ-ent regional and municipal authorities. The financial base of the Bureau has been a topic of ongoing discussion within the organization as some members feel that the Bureau has allowed itself to slip into a position of over-dependency on EU funding. This was brought home forcibly in June 1998 when a number of budget lines, including the one for minority and regional languages, were suspended and ulti-mately suppressed because of a judgement of the European Court of Justice. Fortunately for the Bureau a budgetary provision to support the organisation and the Mercator Centres was included in the 'A' Chapter of the budget thus avoiding a situation which could have led to the total demise of the organisation.

'A rose by any other name'

How should one best describe the languages being 'looked after' by the Bureau? Are they minority languages or regional languages or what? The simple answer is that there is no fully satisfactory or universally acceptable adjective. *Minority* is the most widely used term but it can raise emotive issues or touch on sensitivities in some instances. Catalan may well be a minority language in the context of the Spanish state but it is the majority language on its historical territory in Catalonia, Valencia and the Balearic Islands. Likewise, Irish, while being in a minority position in Ireland today, is very much the majority language in the context of the existence of the Irish people as a literate people. The fact that the Constitution of Ireland defines it as being 'the national language' and 'the first official language' lends the term *minority* a pejorative overtone which it might not have in another context. German is most certainly a minority language in Belgium but it is the most widely spoken language as L1 (Language 1) in the European Union today. The term *regional* is widely used in France and in Italy and seemingly does not offend many people but try calling Welsh a regional language of Britain and wait for the reaction! The Welsh people are a nation you will be told and Welsh is their national language. *Minorisé* or *minorized* is a coinage employed by some people who wish to convey the fact the language in question is not intrinsically *minor* but has been put in a *minority* position as a result of linguistic oppression. It has its advantages but unfortunately is not widely understood nor yet found in dictionaries. One can find terms such as *small, menaced* or *neglected* employed in different circumstances but they tend to convey an image of defensiveness or morbidity – not always inappropriate but nevertheless unhelpful!

The term *lesser used* can be found in the original Hume motion for resolution in 1979. It is by no means perfect, not least grammatically, but it has a number of advantages. It conveys the concept that the language in question is 'lesser used' in the context of the sovereign state in question and side-steps thorny issues as to whether or not the language is somehow less important or less worthy than the majority language of the state or whether or not the territory on which it is spoken should be regarded as a region of the sovereign state or rather the national territory of the people who use the language. Above all, it seems to antagonize few people if any.

Another perennial question is 'what is a language and what is a dialect'? It has to be said that there is no question or doubt concerning most of the languages which fall into the Bureau's remit. Their status as languages is beyond question. However, there are a number of 'borderline cases'. While proponents of these languages angrily refute any suggestion that they are dialects rather than languages in the normal sense of the word, there are others whose criteria for acceptance are not met. The Bureau's position so far has been pragmatic rather than ideological. It has a list of languages which it includes in its membership but no list of 'dialects' which it rejects. Attempts have been made to agree criteria but these have not succeeded. Objectively, one must accept that the status of any given dialect variety can vary because of a range of sociological, political and even financial considerations. No one disputes the existence of a considerable number of Romance languages. However, if one goes back in history one sees that these originated as dialects of Latin. Following on from the collapse of the Roman Empire, political and economic factors ensured that these dialects had different and independent developments. So one must accept that at some point they ceased to be dialects and became what we know today as languages. The same is true for the three extant Q Celtic languages Irish, Scottish Gaelic and Manx Gaelic. The Dutch and the Flemings followed exactly the opposite course and agreed a standard form for what is now their common language – Nederlands. As recently as 1984, Luxembourg decreed that Lëtzebuergesch was its national language although some linguists continued to argue that it was only a German dialect. Germany, in its instrument of ratification of the European Charter for Regional or Minority Languages, accepted Niederdeutsch as a regional language. The Communauté française in Belgium some short years ago issued a decree recognizing Walloon and other *langues d'oïl*. Ulster-Scots is specifically mentioned in the historical 'Good Friday Agreement' which sets out the new political dispensation for Northern Ireland. At the end of the day, perhaps the most important criterion must surely be that of the self-perception of the community in question.

The work of the European Bureau

The Bureau has followed six main strategies in advancing its work – it provides a European forum for those working for the conservation and advancement of lesser used languages; it seeks political and legal support for them; it facilitates an exchange of information and experiences among language activists; it seeks funding and other resources for lesser used language projects; it supports the establishment of ancillary support structures, and it provides a back-up advice and support service for many small linguistic communities.

By establishing broadly representative committees in the member states, it co-ordinates the work of official language promotional agencies, voluntary associations and others working for the different languages with any given state. The value of this in countries like Italy, where there are at least 13 lesser used language communities, or France, where there are eight, should not be underestimated. Joint, well-prepared proposals have been presented to regional and national governments and joint projects have been undertaken. Some member state committees have sub-committees (for example, the UK, France and Spain) as the situation may differ radically from one language situation to another or from one region to another. At European Union level, the Council of the Bureau, comprising two members from each member state committee plus the president, functions as a kind of European lesser used language forum. Again, joint pan-European proposals have been formulated and common positions taken on critical issues. (A very good example of this was the sending of letters on European Language Day 1999 by committees and associations right across Europe to the newly chosen President of the European Commission, Professor Romano Prodi, calling for an EU legal act establishing a multiannual action programme to support lesser used languages.)

Lobbying or advocacy (in more polite parlance) is the main tool in the campaign to obtain legal and political support. The work of the Bureau in the European Parliament and the Council of Europe have been described elsewhere in this chapter but much other work has been achieved at national and regional level: for example, persuading governments to sign the European Charter, enact language legislation, officially recognize linguistic minorities or make provision for the teaching of or teaching through the medium of lesser used languages. Arranging meetings with government ministers, writing to parliamentarians or organizing public rallies are the usual means employed but the Bureau has also been known to participate in street rallies: for example, in support of the Diwan (Breton medium) schools in 1987. The Bureau has also assisted other international organizations in advancing measures to promote lesser used languages. UNESCO and the Bureau collaborated in organizing a highly successful seminar in Luxembourg on the theme 'Lesser Used Languages, Teacher Training and the Culture of Peace' in late 1996. The author was a member of a small expert group, brought together by the Foundation on Inter-Ethnic Relations, to prepare what are now known as the 'Oslo Recommendations regarding the Linguistic Rights of National Minorities'[9] for the OSCE High Commissioner on National Minorities.

It is probably in the field of information exchange that the Bureau has excelled. No two language situations are the same but most share common experiences or problems. Finding out how others have addressed certain issues or overcome certain difficulties can not only be of practical use but can lead to a sense of solidarity and mutual strength. Almost since its inception, the Bureau published a newsletter, *Contact Bulletin*. This appears three times a year and its circulation of 9000 copies reaches readers in all five continents. At one time there were no fewer than five different language editions – French, English, German, Italian and Spanish. Budgetary constraints forced the Bureau to reduce this to one bilingual (French/English) version. *Contact Bulletin* carries reports, not only on the activities of the Bureau, but also on developments in lesser used language circles in general, including book reviews and reports on conferences. An occasional internal newsletter, *Bureau-Info*, is produced in both English and French and is circulated to Bureau members and related organizations.

The Bureau's publications include two series of booklets – the European Languages' series and the Living Languages' series. Both are produced in French and English and some are produced in other languages also. Attractive, full-colour productions, they are intended for the general rather than the specialist reader. The European Languages series describes different language situations. At the time of writing, eight booklets have been produced – 'Vallée d'Aoste – a Range of Resources', 'Scotland, a Linguistic Double Helix', 'North Frisia and Saterland: Frisian between Marsh and Moor', 'Between Alps and Adriatic: the Slovenes in the EU', 'The Sámi – the Indigenous People of Northernmost Europe', 'Yiddish and Judeo-Spanish – a European Heritage', 'Brittany – a Language in Search of a Future' and 'Irish – Facing the Future'. Two other booklets are in preparation – one on the *langues d'oïl* of Belgium and another on Finnish in Sweden.

The Living Languages' series deals with language on the basis of domain. 'The Sound of Europe' deals with the advantages of bilingual education, 'Language Rights, Individual and Collective' with the use of lesser used languages in public administration, 'Images of Europe', with the provision of television services, 'Feeling at Home in your Language', with inter-generational reproduction and 'The Diversity Dividend' with the relationship between language and economy.

Other publications include three databases, dealing with theatre groups, documentation centres and music groups which serve lesser used language communities. 'Key Words' is a glossary of terms used by people engaged in language promotion at European level. The 'Mini-Guide', which resembles the well-known Michelin guides in format, gives a thumbnail sketch of each lesser used language community while 'Funding Possibilities for Minority Language Groups' offers some ideas as to where funding might be found for language projects. The 'Vade-Mecum' is a guide to legal, political and other international documents pertaining to the lesser used languages of Europe while the 'Select Bibliography on Minority Languages in the European Union' offers researchers some useful pointers as to where they may find in-depth information on different language situations. Other publications include a 'European Inventory on Bilingual Educational Systems', a series of posters, three volumes of 'Study Visit Reports', a directory of lesser used language youth organizations and a general information brochure – 'Unity in Diversity' – which has been produced in English, French, German, Italian, Spanish and Dutch. The Bureau has also made two videos, one providing general information and the other dealing with bilingual education. A website has been created at http://www.eblul.org and this is under constant expansion.

The Bureau offers around 80 bursaries each year to language activists to enable them visit another region and see what is being done there to promote the local language. Visits are made in groups, normally of 10 to 12 participants, and preference is given to participants who are deemed to be 'multipliers', that is, well placed to disseminate the information they glean. Over a thousand people have already benefited from this programme and many informal networks have grown out of the contacts made.

The Bureau has organized, usually in association with other bodies, a number of conferences at European, national and regional level. It has always been the policy of the organization to give preference to topics which lend themselves to follow through action. Subject areas covered included various aspects of education, children's publishing as well as newspapers and TV production in lesser used languages.

The main European source of funding for lesser used language projects has undoubtedly been the EU budget line – B3-1006 (Regional Languages and Cultures). Hundreds of projects submitted by lesser used language associations, research institutes, professional bodies (for example, teachers) and language planning agencies have received funding from the EU over the years.[10] Maintaining this line and having it increased year by year has been an important ongoing aspect of the Bureau's work. Helping small associations prepare projects and identify additional sources of funding has also been one of the tasks undertaken by the Bureau. It has also published a small guide for potential applicants.[11] A judgment of the European Court of Justice, which incidentally had nothing to do with language, resulted in the suppression of a number of budget lines, including B3–1006, as they lacked a sufficient legal basis. Some money is still available for lesser used language projects on a provisional basis. The Bureau is currently pressing for the introduction of the necessary legal act to put lesser used language promotion on a firm and ongoing footing.

In 1988, the Bureau, with the moral and financial support of the European Commission, launched a series of information/documentation centres as a support for lesser used language activists. A subsequent withdrawal of support forced the closure of two of these but the three remaining ones – Mercator-Media (Aberystwyth, Wales), Mercator-Law and Legislation (Barcelona) and Mercator-Education (Leeuwarden, Fryslân) – continue to provide an invaluable backup service.

Another support structure, which was forced to cease operating because of a withdrawal of EU financial backing was the Children's European Publishing Secretariat. This was based in Quimper, Brittany in accommodation provided free by the municipal council. This secretariat facilitated and promoted the publication of full-colour children's books in lesser used languages. It did impressive work in its short lifetime.

Another victim of cutbacks was Agora, an Enterprise Information Exchange Centre aimed at promoting economic development in areas where lesser used languages are spoken. It was based in Wales and accommodated by Menter a Busnes, a business consultancy which operates through the medium of Welsh.

Every day the Bureau receives requests for advice, information and practical assistance (for example, providing speakers for conferences, contributing articles for journals). These are dealt with as fully and as promptly as the limited human resources of the Bureau allow. The very fact that there is some place, some person, to whom language activists can turn in moments of crisis or desperation can not only combat a feeling of isolation but can also generate a feeling of collective strength and solidarity.

The European Charter for Regional or Minority Languages

The second edition of *Contact Bulletin*, the Bureau's newsletter, carries on its front page an article entitled 'A significant event'. This rather innocuous and understated heading gives little or no hint of the significance of the developments which would flow from this event. The article described a public hearing, involving over 250 participants, organized in the Palais de l'Europe in Strasbourg by the Standing Conference of Local and Regional Authorities, to discuss what might be done to conserve and promote the regional and minority languages of Europe.[12] In 1981, only nine days before the European Parliament adopted the first Arfé Resolution, the Parliamentary Assembly of the Council of Europe adopted a recommendation on minority languages.[13] Support grew over the following years for the idea of preparing a charter or convention to protect these languages and the public hearing was the first step in sounding out the opinions of those who actually used these languages on a daily basis. It is interesting to note that a photograph, accompanying the aforementioned article, shows no fewer than six members of the Bureau council among the gathering. Following on from this public hearing, the standing conference established a small working group to start drafting the document which we now know as the European Charter for Regional or Minority Languages. Two of the five member working group were members of the Bureau's council – Piero Ardizzone, then President of the Italian Committee and Dr Yvo Peeters of the Belgian Committee. Towards the end of 1987, an advanced draft text was debated. The standing conference extended its consultative process and invited a number of other participants, including the author, to share their views on the draft document. The final draft was presented to the standing conference towards the end of 1987 and was adopted by an overwhelming majority on 16 March 1988. It should be said that opposition to the idea of a charter was expressed forcibly and much work was done by the Bureau in lobbying members of the standing conference so as to allay the fears of some and strengthen the resolve of others.

Following on the vote in the standing conference the draft charter was then sent to the Parliamentary Assembly of the Council of Europe for an opinion. The parliamentary assembly gave a very favourable opinion in October of the same year and the document then faced its greatest hurdle to date – the Committee of Ministers of the Council of Europe. The committee of ministers could either reject, accept or amend the document. In the event, it opted to establish an expert *ad hoc* committee to re-examine the text of the Charter and to make whatever amendments it felt might be necessary in order to achieve a high degree of acceptability. This committee was known as Comité ad hoc langues régionales: CAHLR to use its acronym. Each member state of the Council of Europe, then numbering only 24, was entitled to nominate up to two representatives on the committee. Most member states took an active interest in the draft document and appointed delegations to represent it. The Council of Europe furthermore invited the author to attend meetings of CAHLR as a non-voting observer with the right to speak. CAHLR's work took longer than most of its members had originally anticipated – three years. Every sentence, every word of the Charter was examined and, in a number of instances, amended. It soon became evident that the majority of delegations were generally sympathetic but there were a number of others whose governments had deeply felt reservations about the whole idea of there being a minority languages' charter. Some strong proponents of the Charter were angered and frustrated at, what seemed to them to be, the dilution of certain sections. On the other hand, a pragmatic approach was needed. If the committee of ministers were to vote on the Charter it would require a two-thirds majority to be accepted and abstentions would be counted as negative votes. Most of the delegates took the pragmatic view that a reasonably good Charter which was adopted would be more useful than an excellent one which was rejected. There was another interesting development during the lifetime of CAHLR in that newly-established democracies from Central and Eastern Europe joined the Council of Europe and without exception became involved in the work of CAHLR. It was extremely interesting to note that the three first states – Poland, Hungary and Czechoslovakia – were all very positive in their attitude and made a dramatic appeal to the members of CAHLR for solidarity at the final meeting. Of the then 28 members of the Council of Europe 21 voted in favour of the charter and five abstained. The five abstainees were Greece, Turkey, the United Kingdom, France and Cyprus. (It is also noteworthy that two of these five countries subsequently signed the Charter and a third is about to do so.)

The Charter is an unusual document in many respects. It does not speak of the rights of national minorities or of ethnic groups. It does not speak even of the rights of linguistic communities. It confines itself to languages and their use. Nevertheless, this approach confers very concrete and specific rights on those who use the languages covered by the Charter: on the members of lesser used language communities. The Charter defines 'regional or minority languages' as being languages which are (1) traditionally used within a given territory of a state by nationals of that state who form a group numerically smaller than the rest of the state's population; and (2) different from the official language(s) of that state. It does not include either dialects of the official language(s) of the state or the language(s) of migrants. Interestingly, the Charter may also be applied to an official language which is less widely used on the whole or part of the territory of the contracting state. This provision neatly covers the application of the Charter to Italian in Switzerland and Swedish in Finland, both of which are defined as national and official languages but which undoubtedly occupy a minority position. Part II of the Charter deals with objectives and principles and all contracting parties must accept its provisions. These provisions might be described as ensuring the elimination of any unjustified distinction, exclusion, restriction or preference relating to the use of a regional or minority language or intended to discourage or endanger the maintenance of it. It also requires the contracting parties to apply, *mutatis mutandis*, the principles covered in part II to non-territorial languages, such as the languages of Gypsies and Jews. If part II might be described as reflecting the soul of the Charter, part III could undoubtedly be described as being the flesh and bones. It deals with measures to promote the use of regional or minority languages in public life. It contains seven different articles which deal with domains of life such as education, juridical authorities, administrative authorities in public services, media, cultural activities and facilities, economic and social life and trans-frontier exchanges. Contracting parties are obliged to choose no fewer than 35 paragraphs or sub-paragraphs from this part of the Charter and apply them to the language or languages in question. Three each of these paragraphs or sub-paragraphs must be chosen in respect of the articles on education and cultural activities and facilities respectively. At the time of ratification the contracting party state must state which languages are covered, which paragraphs or sub-paragraphs it has chosen to apply to them and on what territories the provisions will be applied. Within a year of the charter coming into effect as a convention for any given state that state must provide a written report to the Council of Europe on the measures in place to ensure the implementation of the undertaken provisions. Additional reports have to be provided at three-yearly intervals. A special expert committee is appointed to examine each report and submit its own report to the Committee of Ministers of the Council of Europe. Bodies or associations legally established in a state may draw the attention of the Committee of Experts to matters relating to the undertakings entered into by the state. After consulting the state authorities concerned the Committee of Experts may take into account this information in the preparation of its report for the Committee of Ministers. In short, there is an effective, yet fair and balanced, implementation mechanism. Unlike some other international legal instruments, no state could undertake to ratify the Charter and then ignore the implementation of its provisions.

At the time of writing, 20 European countries have signed the Charter – Norway, Finland, Hungary, Denmark, the Netherlands, Luxembourg, France, Spain, Germany, Malta, Cyprus, Liechtenstein, the Ukraine, Romania, Slovenia, the Former Yugoslav Republic of Macedonia, Iceland, Austria, Switzerland and Croatia. Eight of these countries have already ratified it – Norway, Finland, Hungary, the Netherlands, Liechtenstein, Switzerland, Croatia and Germany. The UK finally signed the Charter in March 2000 and it is almost certain that Italy will also sign now that the relevant domestic legislation has passed through the Italian Senate. Sweden is also likely to sign and there are as yet unconfirmed reports of an early instrument of ratification from Denmark. There are also very encouraging signals coming from the Russian Federation which at the present time is sympathetically examining the Charter to see if and how it might implement its provisions. A Russian ratification would be of enormous importance as the Russian Federation recognizes no fewer than 176 national minorities within its frontiers.

The European Charter for Regional or Minority Languages is unique and unparalleled in that it is a legal instrument solely dedicated to the conservation and promotion of lesser used languages. Its warm reception by a majority of independent European states, despite the fact that it is tightly worded and well-focused, augurs well for the future. Members of the Bureau's council and of its secretariat, who played an extremely active role in the preparation of the Charter, can take justifiable pride in what has been attained. The Bureau continues to promote the Charter and looks forward to the time when all member states of the European Union will have signed and ratified it.

Conclusion: looking back – and to the future

How can the work of the European Bureau for Lesser Used Languages be evaluated as an instrument for promoting linguistic human rights? The last 20 years of the twentieth century were in general good years for Europe's minority languages. It is now politically correct to speak of their importance and the rights of those who use them. Linguistic and cultural conservation is slowly but surely becoming as acceptable as the conservation of the physical environment. The European Parliament has adopted four important resolutions on the promotion and conservation of these languages. The UN, UNESCO, the Assembly of European Regions and the OSCE have all adopted political or legal documents supporting them. The Council of Europe has accorded the legal form of a convention to the first ever legal instrument to support lesser used languages. These international legal and political documents have been matched by domestic legislation in many countries and regions. Official language planning agencies have been established in a number of countries, including Wales, Catalonia, the Basque Autonomous Community, Alsace, Ireland and Scotland. It would be a gross exaggeration to say that the European Bureau for Lesser Used Languages brought about these single-handedly. It clearly did not. The aforementioned changes for the better were made possible by developments on the political scene and were brought about because of the perseverance, dedication and vision of a comparatively small number of individuals in lesser used language communities throughout Europe. But it can be said that the European Bureau for Lesser Used Languages was the catalyst which ensured that these forces for change were harnessed and coordinated in a well-focused and effective manner. It provided leadership and vision at a critical juncture, thus ensuring that small linguistic communities did not allow an opportunity – for some of them, their last, had they missed it – slip away.

It may be said that, after 17 years of existence, the Bureau has now completed the first part of its mission and is now entering a new and challenging era. The organization has changed and continues to change. Some changes imposed on it are arguably not for the better. But the resilience of both the organization and its members should not be underestimated. Come what may, the European Bureau for Lesser Used Languages already has one major achievement to its credit. It has proven to small linguistic communities that they can and should act effectively together to safeguard Europe's linguistic and cultural mosaic for coming generations.

Notes

1. Adopted by the General Assembly of the United Nations on 10 December 1948.
2. ILO Convention (No. 107) concerning the protection and integration of indigenous and other tribal and semi-tribal populations in independent countries.

3. Adopted on 14 December 1960 by the General Conference of the UN Educational, Scientific and Cultural Organization.
4. B3-0016/90.
5. Resolution on a Community Charter of Regional Languages and Cultures and on a Charter of Rights of Ethnic Minorities, adopted by the European Parliament on 16 October 1981 (A1-965/80) 16.10.81 OJC 287 p. 57.
6. Resolution on measures in favour of minority languages and cultures. Resolution prepared by Gaetano Arfé and adopted by the European Parliament on 11.03.1983 (A1-1254/82) OJC 68 (14.03.93) p. 104.
7. Resolution on the languages and cultures of regional and ethnic minorities in the European Community adopted by the European Parliament on 30.10.87 (A2-0150/87) OJC 318 (30.11.87) p. 144.
8. Resolution on Linguistic and Cultural Minorities in the European Community adopted by the European Parliament on 9 February 1994 (A3-0042/94) OJC 061 p. 110.
9. Foundation on Inter-Ethnic Relations, The Hague, 1998.
10. See, for instance, Compendium 1995 and Compendium 1996 of projects promoting autochthonous minority languages in the European Union financed by the European Commission (Wynne and Bray) – Brussels, 1998.
11. Funding Possibilities for Minority Language Groups (Bray) Brussels, 1998.
12. Now known as the Congress of Local and Regional Authorities.
13. Recommendation 928 (1981) on the educational and cultural problems of Minority Languages and Dialects in Europe.

Bibliography

Bray, *Funding Possibilities for Minority Language Groups* (Brussels, 1998).
Wynne, and Bray, *Compendium 1995 and Compendium 1996 of Projects Promoting Autochthonous Minority Languages in the European Union Financed by the European Commission* (Brussels, 1998).

3
State Language Ideology and the Shifting Nature of Minority Language Planning on Corsica

Alexandra Jaffe

Introduction

The French nation is well-known for its long history of centralized language policy, and for a language ideology in which French is both the symbol of and the chief medium for the expression of national, civic and cultural identity and legitimacy. French language policy, with its monocultural and monolingual norm, has both devalued local and regional languages and offered powerful economic and cultural rewards for learning French, the only language taught and recognized in France's schools for a good part of the twentieth century. In regions like Corsica, this has resulted in rapid 'language shift' away from the minority language, Corsican. Whereas at the beginning of the twentieth century most Corsicans had Corsican as their mother tongue, by 1950, many Corsicans were French-dominant speakers. Since the 1970s, however, linguistic revitalization movements for many of the minority languages of France arose (Basque, Breton, Occitan in addition to Corsican).

This chapter presents an overview of trends over the last 30 years of Corsican language planning ideology and strategy. Its aim is to explore the way people's ideas about the relationship between language and identity in general, and about the value of minority languages in particular, are shaped by language policies and discourses about language at the state level (and beyond). I argue that the way Corsican language planners sought to raise the status and practice of Corsican in the initial phase of Corsican language revitalization was heavily influenced by French language ideology and linguistic policy, as well as by the cultural and political context of Corsican ethnic nationalism. I go on to document recent popular resistance to language planners' efforts to

reverse the power hierarchy between Corsican and French by empowering Corsican in key public domains (officialization of Corsican and
mandatory Corsican language education in the schools). I argue that
this resistance is also rooted in the experience of language domination
and adherence to a dominant logic in which languages (and identities)
are clearly bounded and have mutually-exclusive identities and values.

The last part of the chapter explores the emergence of new discourses
on language and identity that have been generated in response both to
this popular resistance, and in the context of a widening understanding of the political and cultural contexts defining Corsican identity.
Well before 1992, the notion of 'Europe' began to create new imagined
communities and cultural and economic networks and relationships.
In terms of language policy and planning, the reframing of the relationship with Italy and Italian and other 'Mediterranean' languages in
schools and in the media is discussed, together with the emergence of
a new discourse in the academy that recognizes and validates plural
and heterogeneous forms of language and identity.

Language shift on Corsica

The spread of French and the decline of Corsican, as in many other
places, was precipitated by a combination of factors. The availability of
French education, beginning in the late 1800s (with the Jules Ferry law),
and the economic opportunities it offered provided powerful impetus for
language shift on Corsica. The connection between knowledge of French
and economic advancement was made explicit by teachers. We see this in
Culioli's account of the way his grandfather, a schoolteacher in Corsica
around 1911, represented the value of French to his pupils. Scolding
them for speaking Corsican, he said *'Bande de bourricots! Faites donc un
effort … vous voulez pousser la charrue toute votre vie?'* ['Herd of donkeys!
Make a little effort! Do you want to push a plough all your lives?'] (Culioli
1986, p. 172). Many parents sided with the teachers and accepted that the
better life they wanted for their children required leaving the island and
its language behind.

At the same time as children learned French, they were also schooled
in French-language ideologies, which included normative assumptions
about the link between language and identity, as well as hierarchies of
linguistic and cultural values. First, there was the link between language and citizenship. In the citation above, the same schoolteacher
told his class that *'Plus de quinze mille des nôtres sont dans l'armée.
Comment l'auraient-ils pu s'ils n'avaient pas appris la langue de notre pays,*

la France?' [Over fifteen thousand Corsicans are in the Army. How could they have done this if they had not learned the language of our country, France?] To be a good citizen, one had to speak French, and preferably, 'lose' one's 'patois', for just as French was seen as a vehicle of moral and civic virtue, regional languages were viewed as embodying undesirable cultural traits. An 1880 Army report makes these connections explicit: 'The young Bretons who do not know how to read, write or speak French ... are promptly civilized; they lose the prejudices of their *pays*, abandon native suspicions, and when they return to the village, they are sufficiently frenchified to frenchify their friends by their influence (Weber 1976, p. 299). The language and citizenship link is still strong in French political discourse; one hundred years after the report quoted above, former French Prime Minister Raymond Barre asserted that 'The foremost of the fundamental values of our civilization is the correct usage of our language. There is a moral and civic virtue in the loyal practice of French by the young people' (Bronckart, cited in Luedi 1992, p. 153).

The institutionalization of these ideologies of value made the dominance of French both practical and symbolic. It was practical because French was the language of government, schools and public life. French became, as people said, *la langue du pain* [literally, the language of bread; figuratively, the language with economic value]. It was symbolic because language hierarchy was absorbed by Corsican speakers. This combination of symbolic and practical domination can be glossed as 'diglossia', which I use as a shorthand for compartmentalized, hierarchical relationships between different languages and, specifically, to describe situations in which there is linguistic conflict as a result of language domination/hierarchy (for example, Gardy and Lafont 1981, p. 75; Boyer 1991, pp. 18–23; Marcellesi 1974; Thiers 1987).[1]

It follows that the consequences of language shift are reflected in both language practices and linguistic attitudes. In the early decades of this century, a fair number of Corsican parents who had struggled to learn French as a second language made conscious decisions to speak only French to their children, to give them first language competence in that language. These were also years of intense Corsican outmigration to continental France and to the French colonies. This sped up the process of linguistic assimilation, as did the increased rate of Corsican marriages to non-Corsicans. In 1910, the majority of Corsicans' first language was Corsican. By the 1960s, the balance had begun to tip towards French. And today, it is the rare child whose first language is not French. The effects of language shift and diglossia on practice are not limited to numbers of speakers, however. They include the emergence of contact-induced language varieties and practices. In the Corsican case, these include French that is spoken with varying proportions of Corsican phonological, semantic and syntactic features, Corsican that is spoken with the same kinds of French influences, as well as language alternation/codeswitching.

The attitudinal dimensions of language shift with diglossia are complex. They include the internalization of stigma by minority language speakers, which can be manifested by linguistic insecurity (in French) as well as the devaluation of the minority language. When I first started doing fieldwork in Corsica in the early 1980s, many people characterized Corsican as a 'patois' that was not worth learning (or could not be learned – after all, they would say, it doesn't have a grammar). Diglossia is also manifested as an ideology of oppositional, or compartmentalized values. In other words, because dominant language policy excludes the minority language from the public/ official domain, the minority language gets restricted to informal and intimate contexts of use. This practical restriction is then elevated to an exclusive and oppositional value (in reference to the dominant language). In this logic, the social uses of Corsican are conceptualized as its essential values. Thus, in Corsican metalinguistic discourse, Corsican is represented as the language of the heart and of the hearth, of the warm and informal context of social relations in the village; French on the other hand commands the domain of the formal, the authoritative, the instrumental and intellectual. Neither language is deemed suitable for the other language's functions.

It is important to recognize that this compartmentalization of use and value, while clearly part of a logic and process of linguistic assimilation to the dominant culture, also provided a framework for what I have labelled the 'resistance of separation' (Jaffe 1999). In effect, it reinforced the meaningfulness of an 'alternative' linguistic and cultural market whose capital was cultural solidarity and difference from things French (see Bourdieu 1991; Woolard 1985).

Linguistic revitalization

Beginning in the 1970s, Corsican language activists began to devise strategies to try to reverse the language shift that had occurred. They were profoundly influenced by French linguistic policy, French lan-

guage ideology, Corsican nationalism and their experiences and understandings of the causes of language shift.

It is in regard to the latter issue that Corsican language planners'
understandings of diglossia shaped their revitalization strategies. In
particular, they focused on the relationship between language attitudes
and practices. Corsican was not being transmitted in the home because
it was devalued; part of the reason it was devalued was because it was
not considered a language at all, and because it had no public, official
power or authority. Changing such attitudes was seen as a precondi-
tion for changing behaviours – specifically, encouraging Corsicans to
transmit the language in the home. Early Corsican language activists
embarked on a programme of what the sociolinguist Heinz Kloss
termed 'ausbau' or 'elaboration' of the minority language (see Thiers
1988, p. 91). During the 1970s, strategies of elaboration revolved
around normalization (inserting Corsican into high status domains of
use previously occupied by French alone) and standardization (achievement of linguistic unity, something that was also attributed only to the
dominant language).

As we can see, linguistic elaboration involves making the minority language more 'like' the dominant language in how it is represented and in
its social functions. In this respect, it is ideologically conservative. This
conservatism is understandable in the context of minority language
revitalization. In the Corsican case, there are several reasons why
Corsican language planners were compelled to work within dominant
models of linguistic legitimacy. First of all, these were the models
absorbed by Corsicans through the French school system; they were the
only idiom of language legitimacy people knew. Secondly, there were
pragmatic considerations associated with one of the early goals of
Corsican language planners: to promote the teaching of Corsican in the
schools in order to offset failures of parental transmission. In this effort,
they were highly constrained by contemporary French educational
policy. The 1951 Deixonne law had allowed for the teaching of Alsatian,
Breton and Basque but had excluded Corsican on the grounds that it was
an Italian dialect that was not sufficiently unified or codified to count as a
language. For these reasons, showing that Corsican 'had a grammar',
could be written down, and was distinct from Italian, were central
concerns of early language planners.

The other way that conservative French (and more generally, Western
European) ideologies of language and national identity entered into
Corsican language revitalization movement was via Corsican nationalism. Many language activists were active in or sympathetic to the
nationalist movement – in which Corsican occupied a central role. First,

the existence of Corsican was a pivotal part of Corsican nationalist claims to a distinct culture. In this, the nationalist platform was profoundly influenced (as were other ethnoregionalist movements) by the following tenets of Western European thought about language and political identity: first, that there is (or ought to be) perfect congruence between linguistic, cultural and political boundaries (one language, one people, one nation); second, that those boundaries are 'natural' and impermeable, and enclose internally homogenous systems (Balibar 1991; Hobsbawm 1990; Gal 1992; Handler 1988). In other words, having a language = having a culture = having a right to political self-determination. Secondly, the fact of Corsican language decline was offered as evidence of French policies of 'internal colonialism': of unjustified political, economic and cultural assimilation and domination.

There is a built-in tension in the perspective on the Corsican language I have sketched above. In the context of an essentialist (almost biological) view of the relationship between language and cultural identity, the strength and legitimacy of that cultural identity is called into question when the social practice of the language declines. Language planning that involves revitalization – as it does in Corsica – is thus potentially delegitimizing, since it highlights the fact that members of the society do not all possess the language that is held to be one of the key elements of their individual and collective claims to a particular cultural identity. Below, we will go on to see how this potential for delegitimation operates in popular responses to language legislation.

Three decades of Corsican language planning

The 1970s

The key legislative event of the 1970s was the successful campaign (which included a popular petition) by the linguistic association *Scola Corsa* 'Corsican School' for the inclusion of Corsican under the Deixonne law in 1975. The foundations for this popular support had been laid in the late 1960s and early 1970s by associations such as *Lingua Corsa*, in which young intellectuals living on the continent organized Corsican language classes in cities that had large Corsican populations (Paris, Marseilles, Nice). Much of the momentum for the Deixonne campaign also came from the first of what were to become annual *Ghjurnate Corse* 'Corsican Days' at Corté – political, cultural and linguistic rallies that drew thousands of militant students and nationalist sympathizers. Beginning in 1974, *Scola Corsa* and other linguistic, cultural and political organizations campaigned for a university on the island, and organized yearly 'Summer Universities' at Corté, held on the symbolic grounds of the walled garrison that used to be the headquarters of Pascal Paoli, eighteenth-century 'Father of the Corsican Nation' and founder of the first University of Corsica. The Summer Universities created part of the social momentum that culminated in the opening of the University of Corsica which opened its doors to 500 students in Corté in 1982. Today, over 5000 students attend this university.

In addition to the production of grammars, spelling manuals, lexicons (including two computerized versions) and other pedagogical works, there was a significant Corsican language literary production during the 1970s. *Rigiru* 'Return', a literary magazine edited entirely in Corsican, was founded in 1975. Also in the mid-1970s, the monthly magazine *Kyrn* instituted a Corsican page, which, around 1984, became two pages, until the magazine ceased publication in 1992. Groups like *Canta U Populu Corsu* 'the Corsican People Sing' also played a significant role in the promotion of the language. In these groups, political, cultural and linguistic activism were intertwined: they sang in (and about) Corsican as an expression of a cultural birthright; they revitalized a traditional Corsican polyphonic song form (the *paghjella*); they sang about oppression, resistance and political autonomy. Many of the singers were also politically active in the nationalist movement and/or involved in Corsican language education.

The 1980s

1982 marked the first year of the newly-formed Corsican semi-autonomous Regional Assembly (the first such political body in France). The new political climate and venue was an opportunity for Corsican politicians (on the left, and predominantly from autonomist/ nationalist parties) to launch campaigns for the officialization of Corsican and for mandatory Corsican language education in the schools. These moves are a logical continuation of the effort to reverse the power hierarchy between Corsican and French by empowering Corsican in key public domains.

In 1982, a French Ministry of Education circular allowed for the expansion of the number of weekly hours of voluntary Corsican language instruction and, generally, endorsed a more systematic programme of Corsican language education. Secondary students were allowed to fill language requirements in the curriculum with Corsican, and students taking their *Baccalauréat* (school leaving exam) were able to acquire extra credit points from an optional test in Corsican. The university progressively expanded its offerings in Corsican, and opened a Corsican Studies

Institute. By the late 1980s, degrees in Corsican/ Corsican studies were approved through to the doctorate level.

During this decade, there was a rich production of literary and pedagogical texts. Corsican also became an increasing presence in the broadcast media. In the beginning, the two radio stations broadcasting in Corsican were the *Viva Voce* of the ADECEC (a linguistic association) and RCI (*Radio Corse International*). Neither of these stations could be received outside a limited geographical area. In 1984, Corsica got its own branch of the newly decentralized Radio France: *Radio Corse Frequenza Mora* (RCFM), which has continued to use Corsican extensively in its broadcasts ever since that time. The regional television station, FR3, was moved from Marseilles to Ajaccio, and, under Corsican direction, increased the use of Corsican in its broadcasts.

During the 1980s, three separate motions came before the assembly. The first of these was passed immediately in 1983, and read (my translation):

> The Assembly, having officially recognized the fundamental role of the Corsican language as the cement of culture, and of the urgency of putting into practice a concrete policy of cultural reappropriation which translates the desire of the Assembly to give the people its language back ... has decided to commit itself to a policy of bilingualism, to be implemented in a triennial plan to be elaborated in collaboration with the State. ... In parallel, from now on, the use of the Corsican language will be generalized in the names of places, villages, towns, in the context of news and audiovisual training, as well as in certain public documents.

The practical impact of this resolution was short lived, as it was rejected by then Prime Minister, Mauroy. The assembly was also dissolved a few months later. In 1985, the Castellani Motion called for Corsican language education to be mandatory for the state, and optional for the student. Although this motion was tabled, it was never voted on. In 1989, a motion that would have established Corsican and French as 'co-official', was debated and voted down. I return to these below.

The 1990s

Beginning in 1989, the Corsican Region (represented by the assembly) signed the first of a series of planning contracts with the state. The 1990 contract included a systematic plan for teacher education in Corsican language instruction, provided money for Corsican language laboratories in the Teacher Training Schools, labs and workshops in all secondary schools, the production of pedagogical materials for Corsican language teaching, and a computerized database of the Corsican language.

The 1994 contract included several new initiatives. One was the establishment of 'Mediterranean classes' in two *collèges* (beginning level secondary schools for children aged 12 to 14). In these classes, students study Corsican along with another romance language (Italian or Spanish). Another option allowed students to combine the study of Latin, Corsican and another Romance language. State support was also provided for Corsican language broadcasting on the regional television station, and for continued work on Corsican language databases. As a result of the 1994 contract, four primary schools opened bilingual classes. Labelled 'experimental', these classrooms alternate between Corsican and French throughout the day; French and Corsican are both taught as subjects and are both used as media of instruction (*Cunsigliu Culturale, Suciale è Ecunomicu di a Corsica* 1997, p. 6).

A 1996 survey of Corsican language education conducted by the region showed that 195 out of 24 766 primary school students in Corsica were in fully bilingual classes. Roughly 20 per cent (4870) primary school students received three hours per week of Corsican language instruction. The remainder (approximately 75 per cent) had one hour a week of Corsican. In secondary schools, 35 per cent of the students in *collèges*, 13 per cent of *lycée* (high school) students and 30 per cent of students in vocational high schools were taking Corsican classes. About a third of all students taking the *Baccalauréat* elected to take a test in Corsican. At the University of Corsica, all students are required to take between one and one and a half weekly hours of Corsican.

These thumbnail sketches of minority language elaboration on Corsica demonstrate some significant gains in minority language normalization and standardization. The successes of Corsican language planning have a number of sources. In the political sphere, the expanded public and educational use of Corsican has profited from the shift to the left in French national politics. This shift paved the way for greater national recognition and support for minority cultures and language rights, and was accompanied by decentralizing policies that facilitated institutional applications of those rights in regions like Corsica. Political decentralization made the Regional Assembly possible, and the presence of this assembly allowed Corsican nationalists to seek election, and once elected, to operate within a 'mainstream' political framework, where they have kept language issues at the forefront. At the same time, internal fragmentation in the nationalist fold has also allowed the general public to recognize and lend their support to 'moderate' autonomists, who have supported linguistic and cultural rights but distanced themselves from the violence of the armed underground nationalist movement. For there have been junctures where nationalist promotion of Corsican has actually created a popular backlash, in which people who rejected nationalist politics felt obliged to withhold support from Corsican language promotion.

But what of the original goals of Corsican activists: to increase the number of Corsican speakers, to slow, stop and even reverse the process of language shift? Here, the results are mixed. On the one hand, normalization strategies have created dramatic shifts in sociolinguistic judgements about Corsican's status as a language. Few Corsicans will say that Corsican is 'not a language', and the word 'patois' is no longer heard. I would argue that 'normalization' strategies – such as literary corpus building and the generalization of language teaching in the schools – have had a slow but significant symbolic effect, and have persuaded many Corsicans of the linguistic legitimacy of the language. In other words, Corsican now has higher social standing within the dominant model of language legitimacy.

There is no doubt that these changes of attitudes are preconditions for language revitalization. But the effect of attitudes on practices has neither been immediate nor dramatic. It is fair to say that language planning in Corsica to date has failed to mobilize Corsicans on a grand scale to take aggressive action to protect the minority language. Most Corsican speakers, even if appreciative of Corsican, speak French to children. And in regard to Corsican language education, while parents have seldom tried to undermine the teaching of Corsican, they have also seldom played an aggressive role in demanding Corsican courses. This passive acceptance of Corsican schooling has been accompanied by a fairly active resistance to legal mandates for that education. Let me return briefly to the political context, and the language legislation efforts of the 1980s to explain and connect these popular attitudes.

The debate over mandatory Corsican

In order to try to understand the inability of the Corsican Regional Assembly to pass legislation making Corsican the official (or co-official) language on Corsica and an obligatory subject in the schools, I have analysed transcripts of assembly debates on language legislation as well as interview and survey data on support for mandatory Corsican education collected during 1988–89 (Jaffe, in press). Those who supported making Corsican mandatory (politicians and the general public) argued from what will now be familiar positions. Some took an 'essentialist' view of the relationship between language and identity, arguing that official status and mandatory teaching of Corsican was a cultural birthright. For some survey respondents, cultural and political rights were intertwined: *'Comment peut-il avoir un Peuple Corse sans l'affirmation et l'expression de sa langue? Comment parler de la culture corse sans parler de la langue corse?'* [How can you have a Corsican People without the affirmation and expression of its language? How can you speak of Corsican culture without speaking about the Corsican language?] Others advocated mandatory Corsican as a way of sidestepping the problem of unsupportive or apathetic parents. In other words, they supported language education as a way of re-establishing an authentic societal relationship with the language they considered the vector of Corsican culture. Another subset of respondents supported making Corsican a school requirement because of the symbolic authority and legitimacy associated with the institution of the school. Like language planners, they thought that language status (or power) had a positive effect on language attitude, and commented that official, mandatory status for Corsican would convince parents and students that the language was being taken seriously, and prompt them to take it seriously as well. As one of the respondents wrote, *'Le choix des sujets optionnels est fait le plus souvent pour des raisons utilitaires. Si le corse reste optionnel, il continuera à être peu choisi et disparaîtra'.* [The choice of optional subjects is most often made for utilitarian reasons. If Corsican remains optional, it will continue to not be chosen (since its value is not utilitarian) and will disappear.]

Many of those who opposed mandatory Corsican also embraced an essentialist view of the language:identity connection, which we have identified as a legacy of dominant language ideology. In this, they were not different from many supporters. What distinguishes opponents of mandatory Corsican is that they anchored an essentialist position to a diglossic, oppositional model of language value. The most frequently cited reason for opposing mandatory bilingualism was an objection to any limits on freedom of choice. They located the value of Corsican language and culture in the individual's voluntary choice to speak the language. This sentiment is a logical outcome of the experience of diglossia: as we have seen, few corsophones have learned Corsican outside the voluntary, affective domain, and Corsican is important to them because it is not imposed like French (see McDonald 1989, p. 154). This makes sense of one Corsican politician's assertion in the 1985 debate on the Castellani bill, that he had the impression that he was contributing to the death of his mother tongue. It also explains why learning Corsican in school was viewed by some people as a cont-aminating, de-authenticating act (see Jaffe 1993a), and why some of these respondents thought that requiring Corsican would have a nega-tive effect on student motivation. One person summed this up by writing, '*Toute imposition est la source de résistance.*' [Every imposition is a source of resistance.]

To summarize, reactions to language planning legislation illustrate what Eckert has called the 'paradox' of minority language revitalization movements (Eckert 1993). That is, for a variety of practical and ideo-logical reasons, language planning strategies often fail to challenge the fundamental assumptions – and thus the structures of power and value – of dominant language ideology. This means that language planning strategies themselves will tend to be evaluated from within those structures of thought and feeling, and may not be readily accepted by ordinary speakers, since they blur the (limited) distance from domina-tion afforded by the separate (though unequal) minority language market.

New perspectives on Corsican language and identity: towards a plural model

Over the last ten years, Corsican language activists have responded to the kinds of negative reactions to language planning exemplified by the lack of strong public support for official and mandatory status for Corsican. In this final section, the emergence of new discourses on language and identity that attempt to transcend the French–Corsican contrast set will be explored. Well before 1992, the notion of 'Europe' began to create new imagined communities and cultural and econ-omic networks and relationships and these in turn have influenced language policy and planning. First, there follows a discussion on the reframing of the relationship with Italy and Italian and other 'Mediterranean' languages in the schools and in the media, and second, the notion of 'polynomy', which has replaced diglossia as the organizing theme of academic characterizations of language practice and ideology.

Relations with Italy and Italian

In the early days of Corsican language revitalization, Corsican's fragile status as a language made it very important to differentiate Corsican from Italian, its closest linguistic partner. In the framework of normative assumptions about the relationship between language and identity, any reference to linguistic similarity with Italian could provide a threat to

Corsican's claim to having a unique linguistic identity and a legitimate status as a language. In the academic context, it is clear that some italianists ascribed subordinate status to Corsican, tolerating it as an oral variant of the dominant language but not supporting Corsican literacy or education. In the context of the struggle for legitimacy, school resources and students, it also made sense not to support the teaching of Italian, since it was seen as being in direct competition with Corsican.[2] For these reasons, I was taken somewhat by surprise by a 1989 manifesto supporting the teaching of Italian, signed by almost 100 Corsican cultural and linguistic activists. The manifesto advocated 'renewing' cultural and linguistic links with the 'other continent'. Some subsequent applications of this general perspective can be seen in the media and in the academic context. In the academic sphere, we can point to collaboration between the University of Corsica and Sardinian scholars on issues of language and culture under the European Union Interregional Programme. There have also been some interesting initiatives in radio broadcasting. In the summer of 1991, RCFM ran a regular feature in which an Italian correspondent phoned in from various cities in Tuscany (the region closest to Corsica by boat), describing the surroundings and cultural events to would-be Corsican tourists. What is significant is the assumption of intelligibility: the correspondent spoke in untranslated Italian. In other words, it assumed a listening audience that was competent in Corsican, and assumed that Corsican and Italian were mutually intelligible. This assumption is neither correct nor incorrect; it is a matter of perspective. Just as the same glass of water can be seen as half full or half empty, Corsican and Italian can be seen as different enough to pose an obstacle to communication or similar enough to make communication possible. More recently, in 1998, RCFM broadcast a dramatic mini-series about the life of the eighteenth-century figure Pascal Paoli. The depicted characters (with historical accuracy) speak Corsican, Italian and French. And as a final example here, Italian has entered the school curriculum as a 'partner' language to Corsican in the 'Mediterranean' sections of some of the Corsican middle schools mentioned above.

   There are several ways in which we can explain this emergence of a new pro-Italian voice. First, it can be taken as index of Corsican language activists' increased confidence in the general public's recognition and acceptance of Corsican's status as a language. Second, it represents a strategic response to Corsican–French diglossia: endorsing Italian language teaching, and emphasizing the cultural connections to Italy is a way of escaping the pervasive opposition of Corsican and French and counterbalancing the effects of French linguistic and cultural domination by introducing a new, 'powerful' cultural and linguistic partner. Finally, as asserted above, the pro-Italian position is linked to new ways of conceptualizing Corsican identity within a wider framework than that of the French nation. The European Union, both as an idea and as a policy-making body distributing economic resources, has been a significant catalyst for this process. The Interregional Programme, designed to promote economic and cultural exchange between neighbouring regions, is one such example. The development of European-wide coalitions of island and 'peripheral' regions is another (see Jaffe 1993b). In other words, being 'not-French' in this context does not necessarily imply a loss of identity or of partnerships.

Polynomy: a plural view of language identity

In 1990, the Corsican Studies Institute of the University of Corsica organized a conference around the theme of 'polynomic languages'. The sociolinguist Marcellesi coined this term in 1989, and defines it as 'a language with an abstract unity, recognized by its users in several modalities of existence; all of them are equally tolerated and they are not ranked or functionally specialized. It is accompanied by phonological and morphological intertolerance between users of different varieties; moreover, lexical multiplicity is seen as a source of richness' (1989, p. 170, my translation). He characterized Corsican as 'very' polynomic, since Corsicans did not stigmatize linguistic variability, but rather, embraced an ideology of 'unity in diversity'. Since 1990, Corsican academics have actively promoted this image of Corsican language unity. This new discourse is an interesting and significant shift from the public dissemination by intellectuals of the term 'diglossia' in the early 1980s. Talking about diglossia had focused attention on the power of the dominant language; it explained language practices (including those which disfavoured Corsican) in terms that situated individual choices within a matrix of social forces. It exhorted Corsicans to undo diglossia both by speaking Corsican and by practicing and promoting literacy in Corsican. In contrast, the concept of polynomy does not advocate a power reversal, but, rather, a redefinition of what power The discourse of 'diglossia', while critical of the techniques of language domination, nevertheless represented diglossic language attitudes and practices as undesirable: they were something Corsicans were urged to shed. In contrast, the discourse of polynomy represents Corsicans as a superior speech community measured against new norms of inclusivity and tolerance – not only for different regional varieties of Corsican but also, for the mixed codes that result from language contact.

This new, plural, social constructionist ideology of language identity is not without its critics, nor is it always easy to apply. This is because dominant language ideologies die hard, both in the popular imagination and in institutional contexts such as the school, where a long prescriptivist tradition with regard to language is inscribed in curriculum, testing and social practices (see Jaffe 1999, Chapter 5). Nevertheless, it represents a significant step in Corsican language activists' attempts to change the terms of engagement rather than simply trying to play as equals on linguistic and ideological terrain defined by the more powerful.

To summarize, the Corsican case shows how local ideas about the relationship between language and identity are shaped by extralocal forces. In the early days of Corsican language revitalization, language planning strategies were formulated in direct response to state language ideologies and policies. More recent language planning strategies have been influenced both by the idea of the new Europe as well as by Corsican language planners' understandings of the way that state ideologies have affected Corsicans' internalized beliefs about identity and language. The history of Corsican language activism also shows that minority language planning is never just a straightforward question of promoting the use of a minority language. It is inevitably about defining and redefining the very concept and content of identity – local, regional, ethnic, national and supranational – and how identity is linked to linguistic codes.

Notes

1. See Tollefson 1983 and Hudson's preface to his 1992 bibliography on diglossia for a discussion of variation and debate in the use of the term diglossia.
2. There are also historical reasons why the Corsican–Italian connection has been de-emphasized, including the low status of Italian migrant workers in Corsica in the nineteenth century, as well as the association of pro-Italian cultural politics with Mussolini's interwar efforts to 'reclaim' lost cultural/linguistic territories of Italy.

Bibliography

Balibar, E. 'The Nation Form: History and Ideology', in I. Wallerstein and E. Balibar eds, *Race, Nation, Class: Ambiguous Identities* (New York: Routledge, Chapman and Hall, 1991) pp. 86–106.

Bourdieu, P. *Language and Symbolic Power* John B. Thompson ed., Trans. G. Raymond and M. Adamson (Cambridge: Polity Press, 1991).

Boyer, H. *Langues en conflit: études sociolinguistiques* (Paris: L'Harmattan, 1991).

Culioli, G.X. *La terre des seigneurs* (Paris: Lieu Commun, 1986).

Cunsigliu Culturale, Suciale è Ecunomicu di a Corsica. Lingua (Publications de l'Assemblée de Corse 1997).

Eckert, P. 'The Paradox of National Language Movements', *Journal of Multilingual and Multicultural Development* (4)4, (1983) 289–300.

Gal, S. 'Multiplicity and Contention Among Ideologies: a Commentary', *Pragmatics* 2(3), (1992) 445–50.

Gardy, P. and Lafont, R. '*La diglossie comme conflit: l'exemple occitan'*, *Languages* 61, (1981) 75–91.

Handler, R. *Nationalism and the Politics of Culture in Quebec* (Madison: University of Wisconsin Press, 1988).

Hobsbawm, E.J. *Nations and Nationalism since 1780* (New York: Cambridge University Press, 1990).

Hudson, A. 'Diglossia: a Bibliographic Review', *Language in Society* 21(4), (1992) 611–55.

Jaffe, A. The Question of Obligation: Authority and Authenticity in Corsican Discourse about Bilingual Education, in M. Martin-Jones and M. Heller, eds, *Voices of Authority: Education and Linguistic Diversity* (Ablex, in press).

Jaffe, A. *Ideologies in Action: Language Politics on Corsica* (Berlin: Mouton de Gruyter, 1999).

Jaffe, A. Obligation, Error and Authenticity: Competing Cultural Principles in the Teaching of Corsican?, *Journal of Linguistic Anthropology* 3(1), (1993a) 99–114.

Jaffe, A. Corsican Identity and a Europe of Peoples and Regions, in T. Wilson and E. Smith, eds, *Cultural Change and the New Europe: Perspectives on the European Community* (Boulder, CO: Westview Press, (1993b)), pp. 61–80.

Luedi, G. French as a Pluricentric Language, in M. Clyne ed., *Pluricentric Languages* (New York: Mouton de Gruyter, 1992), pp. 149–77.

Marcellesi, J.-B. *Introduction à la sociolinguistique* (Paris: Larousse, 1974).

Marcellesi, J.-B. and Gardin, B. Corse et théorie sociolinguistique: reflets croisés', in G. Ravis-Giordani ed., *L'île miroir* (Ajaccio: La Marge, 1989), pp. 165–74.

McDonald, M. *We Are Not French* (New York: Cambridge University Press, 1989).

Thiers, J. Idéologie diglossique et production de sens, *Peuples Méditerranéens* 38 (1987) 139–54.

Thiers, J. *Epilinguisme et langue polynomique: L'exemple Corse.* Unpublished Doctoral Dissertation, Université de Rouen, 1988.

Tollefson, J.W, Language Policy and the Meanings of Diglossia, *Word* 34 (1983) 1–9.

Weber, E. *Peasants Into Frenchmen* (Stanford: Stanford University Press, 1976).

Woolard, K. 'Language Variation and Cultural Hegemony: Toward an Integration of Sociolinguistic Theory and Social Theory, *American Ethnologist* 12, (1985) 738–48.

4
'Catalan is Everyone's Thing': Normalizing a Nation

Susan DiGiacomo

> Language is … a natural product, not the result of convention or of human artifice. … Attempting to reform a language as we would change a law is a ridiculous undertaking: to purge it of idioms is to rob it of its original features, to disfigure it instead of embellishing it.
>
> Enric Prat de la Riba, *La nacionalitat catalana*, 1978 (1906), p. 76; my translation[1]

Introduction: language and nation

I begin with this quotation from the work of the great theoretician of Catalan nationalism, Prat de la Riba (1870–1917), because it points to the ambiguity with which language, as the premier symbol of Catalan national identity, is now and has historically been suffused. For Prat, authentic nations are natural communities of action, thought and speech. Continuities of practice – especially linguistic practice – represented as timeless, unchanging and natural, constitute the fact of difference (*el fet diferencial*) that legitimizes aspirations to self-government. Yet, paradoxically, the naturalness of language as the highest expression of nationhood and instrument of political sovereignty is belied by a long history of efforts to standardize the language and normalize its use. Ironically, the institutionalization of a new standard was initiated by Prat himself in one of his first official acts as the newly elected president of the Diputació Provincial (provincial administration) of Barcelona in 1907. He created the Institut d'Estudis Catalans (Institute of Catalan Studies) and charged it with the responsibility for scientific investigation in three areas: history and archaeology, the sciences, and philology. A modern nation, Prat reasoned, required a modern language in which to conduct its affairs. Catalan science should also be science *in Catalan*.

Jacqueline Urla (1988, 1993) has argued with reference to the Basque case that language planning is anything but a 'natural' outgrowth of nationalism. It rests upon the legitimacy of quantified knowledge and the modern concept of population, the well-being of which is thought to depend on scientific study and management in many domains – including public health and education, crime control and urban planning. The modern welfare state generally enjoys a monopoly on the deployment of these 'techniques of power' (Foucault 1982, p. 212), but as Urla points out (1993, p. 837), it is a mistake to assume that quantification is always a form of domination. By strategically appropriating statistical measurement, Basque language activists have not only found a way to resist the Spanish state – with its own devices of control – but to decentre scientific expertise and challenge the validity of the Basque government's own language planning efforts.

Similar shifts in Catalan subjectivity occurred over the course of the twentieth century. In this chapter I will argue that the academic discipline of philology has come to constitute a metadiscourse on national authenticity in Catalonia, though in a way that has been far from uniform, or uniformly accepted. Contradiction and contestation have been central features of it from the beginning and this continues to be the case – and it is to this dissonance that I wish to draw attention. This indeterminacy arises out of the subversive nature of resistance strategies. They are not made up out of whole cloth, but are instead made up of a patchwork of values and practices appropriated from dominant structures and discourses, and invested with new meanings.

In a similar way, threads from the past are incorporated into the design, with strategic embellishments and erasures. In his essay *Imagined Communities*, Benedict Anderson (1983, p. 15) quotes Ernest Renan to the effect that a national community is defined not only by what its members share in common, but by the things they have collectively forgotten. As Lass (1988) has shown for the Czech case, a collective sense of history depends on its periodic erasure and the selective recovery of 'lost' traditions. As the state historicizes only certain ranges of culture and social structure and represents them as total and authentic, so also do stateless nations invoke the past selectively, reviving 'forgotten' history in a counter-hegemonic process. The emergent identities forged in this process are not, however, immune to alternative readings of the alternative record.

The following sections of this chapter explore these ideas with reference to language ideology, practice and identity in Catalonia. First, a brief social history of the Catalan language is presented in order to highlight the sources of different understandings of Catalonia as a language community. The next two sections, drawing on fieldwork in Barcelona since 1977, analyse contemporary language ideologies and ground the political debate on language planning in a specific social context: the classroom instruction of Catalan for adult students, where language ideology and language practice daily confront each other, confounding both official and popular notions of authentic speech and identity. The conclusion explores the implications of the Catalan case for theories of nationalism.

The Catalan language in social historical context

Since national languages and literatures both require and demonstrate time depth and historical continuity, they are legitimizing symbols for many nationalist movements. Both literary and literal, they are concretizing proof of the existence and durability of the nation. Catalans are fond of referring to *la nostra llengua mil.lenària* – our thousand-year-old language – and proudly point to the earliest surviving texts in Catalan: the Homilies d'Organyà, a collection of sermons that dates to the twelfth century. An implicit comparison is embedded in this discourse about the antiquity of Catalan: it is no less ancient, and no less literary, than Castilian, the language of the Spanish state.

Historical linguistics places the emergence of spoken Catalan at about 800 AD (Duarte and Massip 1981, p. 23), roughly the same time that the other Romance languages were forming as a result of contact between Latin and local languages. It was neither a derivative nor a dialectal variant of Castilian, nor was it simply an oral vernacular, but developed a distinct literary standard and an extensive history of literary use that began not – as with most Romance languages – with poetry, but with prose, the thirteenth-century novels and theological works of the philosopher Ramon Llull being among the earliest examples. At its height, the Catalan literary tradition produced such masterpieces as Joanot Martorell's 1490 novel of chivalry, *Tirant lo blanc*, a book whose merits were praised extravagantly by Cervantes through a character in *Don Quijote*. The priest who conducts an inquisition over the contents of the knight's library chooses *Tirant lo blanc* as the only book of its kind to be spared from burning, exclaiming, 'Give it to me, friend, for to my mind that book is a rare treasure of delight ... for its style it is the best book in the world' (Cervantes 1604 [J.M. Cohen, trans., 1950], p. 60).

The emerging Catalan nationalist movement of the mid-nineteenth century, like many other such movements, initially took the form of a literary revival that ended three centuries of disuse (*la decadència*). Language was represented as a great abandoned tradition, a national treasure that had waxed with the fortunes of the medieval Catalan mercantile empire, and waned at the end of the fifteenth century as the locus of power and economic centre of gravity began to shift away from Catalonia and towards Castile. The emergent urban aristocracy differentiated itself from its social inferiors by adopting Castilian, a process hastened by the establishment of a Castilian-speaking court in Valencia in the early sixteenth century (Amelang 1986, pp. 193–5; see also Duarte and Massip 1981, pp. 86–7, and López del Castillo 1987, p. 65). By the seventeenth century, Castilian had become an instrument of political domination in the hands of absolutist Spanish monarchs (see Elliott, 1963, p. 322), and the final blow came in 1714, at the end of the Spanish War of Succession. Philip V's decree of the Nueva Planta, or 'New Plan,' of 1716 did away with all of Catalonia's independent institutions of government, culture and learning. In 1779, a Catalan resident in Madrid wrote – in Castilian – of the demise of his 'antique provincial language' in the face of the new 'republic of letters' (Capmany, cited in Vallverdú 1979, p. 35). For the educated classes of the time, Catalan had become degenerate and plebeian, a language of illiterate peasants, servants and artisans.

What is wrong with this picture? It is not inaccurate, but it is incomplete, a partial view from the metropole – which is where literary Catalan would be 'rediscovered' in the nineteenth century. As Peter Sahlins' research has shown, in towns and villages distant from larger urban areas, Catalan remained not only the spoken language of local society but its written language as well. Although the registers of the Pyrenean municipality of Puigcerdà switched abruptly from Catalan to Castilian in 1720, 'medical works, technical manuals, educational texts, ... religious tracts, notarial registers, and private contracts all continued to be written and published in Catalan' (Sahlins 1989, p. 126; see also Sahlins 1998, pp. 33, 51). The *decadència* is thus something of a misnomer, but perhaps a necessary one. As Lass (1988, p. 467) has argued, 'history (like memory) depends on the cultural production of absence'. The *decadència*, during which the Catalan language had lain buried for some 300 years in 'the folk', was just such a culturally constructed lapse of memory, a 'hiatus in which a recontextualization could be claimed' (Lass 1988, p. 459).

The rediscovery of Catalonia's national literary heritage is conventionally dated to 1833, when Bonaventura Carles Aribau's ode 'La Pàtria' was published. Aribau writes as one living, through chance and circumstance but not by choice, in Madrid. His 'fatherland' appears in the initial verses to reside in the beauty of the Catalan landscapes whose loss he laments so profoundly that 'fruits lose their sweetness and flowers their perfume' (Castellet and Molas 1979, p. 139). But halfway through the poem he locates his sense of identity in more intimate terms: 'What does it matter if a trick of destiny has brought me/to view the towers of Castile from close by/if my ear is not deaf to the troubadour's song/nor in my breast a noble memory fail to awaken to its strains?' (Castellet and Molas, 1979, p. 139). The medieval stories of kings and sages sung in *llemosí* (Limousin, a poetic reference to Catalano-Provençal) become a highly personal link not only to a heroic past, but to Aribau's own past. He imbibes the language of those distant forebears in his mother's milk – 'In accents Limousin sounded my first infant's wail' – and now, 'When I find myself alone, in dialogue with my soul,/I speak in Limousin, for it knows no other tongue' (Castellet and Molas, 1979, p. 140). Aribau's romantic vision both naturalizes and historicizes the linkage between the true self, language and nation.

The medieval glories celebrated in Aribau's verses came to be experienced as real and authentic, and their connection to the present as self-evident, in part through being memorialized in a kind of living monument to the language: the *Jocs Florals*, or Floral Games. These public poetry competitions of medieval origin were established in 1859 under the sponsorship of the Barcelona city government, and re-enacted yearly.

Not everyone, however, was pleased. The literary critic Josep Yxart, writing about the *Jocs Florals* of 1875, commented witheringly on the convoluted style employed by contestants who 'would not content themselves with lovingly disinterring the rustiest of archaic usage, but endeavoured to disguise words as such: *new archaisms*!' (Yxart 1980 [1887], p. 218; emphasis in the original). In fact, controversy broke out almost immediately after the first *Jocs Florals*. The very next year, in 1860, the Catalan playwright Frederic Soler (who was and is known primarily by his pseudonym, Serafí Pitarra) and a group of like-minded colleagues publicly pronounced themselves in favour of a literary language as close as possible to *el català que ara es parla*: 'the Catalan we speak now'. This kind of linguistic partisanship reflected shifting class structures in nineteenth-century Barcelona, as the old patrician class gave way to the new industrial elite whose wealth supported the revitalization of Catalan social, cultural and political life (McDonogh 1986).

A modern writer, Xavier Fàbregas, has characterized this conflict of language ideologies as a 'polemic to be grasped with tweezers', gingerly, for it is far less straightforward than it appears to be. Though the stilted *jocfloralista* model of Catalan reached (and sometimes strained) for authenticity through archaism, while *el català que ara es parla* cheerfully embraced the inevitable Castilianisms that had crept into the language over three centuries of linguistic subordination (Solà 1980, p. 48; Duarte and Massip 1981, pp. 86–8), they resembled each other much more than either party wanted to admit. Both sides claimed the uncontaminated waters of Valencian Renaissance poetry as their source, though neither possessed precise criteria for what constituted acceptable usage (Fàbregas 1980, p. 44). In the late nineteenth and early twentieth centuries, the works of such figures as the playwright Àngel Guimerà and the novelist Narcís Oller helped to anchor Catalan literary production in contemporary speech and social reality, a trend reflected in the movement of political ideas from regionalist to openly nationalist (Ferrando and Nicolás 1993, pp. 159–60).

In the work of the philologist Pompeu Fabra, and in Prat's 1907 decision to place in his hands the task of developing a modern Catalan standard, we can discern the transition between the romantic vision of language, nation and identity and a new kind of subjectivity rooted in scientific discourse. In a 1913 speech on the occasion of the publication by the Institut d'Estudis Catalans of the first of Fabra's great works, his *Orthographic Rules*, Prat's view of language as a natural reflection of the national spirit can be seen giving way to a new sense of the potential dangers of allowing natural processes to go unregulated. 'A language in its natural state', he wrote,

> without literary cultivation, comes to be a collection of dialects, a system of different language forms, heterogeneous though linked by a certain unity of grammatical laws. The untrained or hasty observer thinks that he sees before him different languages; because the phonetics, the lexicon, the word endings all vary. Only the philological researcher can discover beneath the luxuriant variety the internal unity that permits classification of all these language forms as dialectal variants of a single language. [Prat de la Riba 1978 (1913), p. 149]

This is the voice not of the romantic poet, but of the natural historian, the scientist.

Seen in historical context, the change of tone becomes less surprising. A year after this speech, in 1914, the four provincial administrations (*diputacions*) of Catalonia were consolidated into a single administrative unit called the Mancomunitat, over which Prat presided until his death in 1917, and which continued to function until the dictatorship of Primo de Rivera abolished it in 1925. The forerunner of the restored Generalitat (the Catalan autonomous government), the Mancomunitat embarked on a broad range of social, cultural and infrastructural programmes that included educational reform through the introduction of innovative pedagogical techniques grounded in developmental psychology, modernization and expansion of the technical and professional colleges (Ardit *et al.*, 1980, p. 439), and an ambitious design for an integrated system of health care that included up-to-date psychiatric services (Comelles 1991, p. 200).

Under the authority of the Mancomunitat, the Institut d'Estudis Catalans published Fabra's *Orthographic Dictionary* (1917) and his *Catalan Grammar* (1918). These elevated Fabra the philologist to Fabra the national hero and, taken together, they constitute a kind of textual monument to the nation. It is with Fabra that the word 'normalization' enters the vocabulary of Catalan language politics. In a 1929 essay, he uses the word in the grammarian's sense – 'we have come to possess a set of generally accepted grammatical rules' (Fabra 1980 [1929], p. 177) – but there is no doubt of the political intent behind the scholarship. In an earlier essay he points out that 'while Catalan remained a language lacking a unified and fixed orthography, lexicon and grammar, it could not be introduced into the schools nor could it aspire to official uses', and goes on to describe the use of these new rules as a patriotic duty incumbent upon Catalan writers (Fabra 1980 [1915], pp. 138, 40).

Fabra's works are still the foundation on which later dictionaries and models of usage have been constructed. He envisioned a standard Catalan flexible enough to be a language of science and government as well as of poetry, and for this reason he kept it as close as possible to *el català tal com se parla* (Fabra, 1891, cited in Solà 1980, p. 53). 'The goal we are pursuing', Fabra wrote (cited in Solà 1977, p. 71),

> is not the resurrection of a medieval language, but the formation of the modern language that would have emerged from our ancient

tongue without the long centuries of literary decadence and subordination to a foreign language.

In characterizing his task as the scientific reconstruction of natural
processes of change, Fabra was implicitly invoking the concept of evolution. If what Lass (1988) has called the 'meaning-fulfilment of
history' was accomplished in nineteenth-century nationalist movements by romantic documents and political monuments, with the turn
of the twentieth century it is science that assumes this concretizing,
meaning-fulfilling function.

National reconstruction and language planning

Fabra's *General Dictionary of the Catalan Language* was published in
1932, the same year that Catalonia's indigenous political institutions
were restored through the Statute of Autonomy under the Second
Spanish Republic, and language planning, in concept if not in name,
began in earnest (Galí 1979, pp. 60ff). This process was cut short after
four years, with the outbreak of the Spanish Civil War in 1936, and
after Franco's victory in 1939 the dictatorship made every effort to
erase all traces of Catalan not only from public life, but from many
aspects of private life as well (Benet, 1978; Ferrer i Gironès 1985). The
Franco regime lasted until 1975, although by the late 1960s the laws
against the public use of Catalan were no longer being enforced as
thoroughly as they had been during the previous two decades.
Nonetheless, two generations of Catalans had grown up in a society in
which the language of school, workplace, commerce, the mass media
and government was Castilian.

Moreover, Catalan society had changed radically since the war.
Hundreds of thousands of people fled the poverty of rural southern Spain
to seek a living in the industrial north. By 1970, well over half of the
3 million inhabitants of the densely populated Barcelona metropolitan
area had been born outside Catalonia (Recolons 1979). The Franco
regime's prohibition on the public use of Catalan ensured that these
'immigrants' had few opportunities to learn Catalan. The language barrier
between natives and newcomers was made especially pernicious by the
fact that it paralleled class cleavages: the Catalan- speaking natives tended
to be middle-class, while the Castilian-speaking immigrants tended to be
working-class.

In the 1977 elections to the Spanish parliament, the Cortes, these
'other Catalans' (Candel 1964), largely voted with the progressive

Catalan middle class for the Spanish Socialist Workers' Party and its coalition partners, the Catalan Socialist Party, whose campaign successfully linked questions of social justice with the restoration of Catalan autonomy. Although a centre-right coalition won the majority, the socialists emerged as the main opposition party. Anticipating victory in the next general elections, the Catalan socialists began positioning themselves to share power in Madrid. Attentive to the reception of their message there as well as among their working-class supporters at home, the Catalan socialists went on to argue for a bilingual strategy of normalization when the political arena shifted to the Catalan parliamentary elections in 1980. A highly selective use of memory and history stressed the articulation of a Catalan national society on the basis of class solidarity and the rights of individual citizens, rather than as a language community. In fact, the issue of language communities was deliberately blurred by characterizing Catalonia as 'one community that speaks two languages', a formulation that suggested a naturally-occurring bilingualism rather than the diglossic and codeswitching language use patterns that were the consequence of post-Civil War repression (see DiGiacomo 1986).

   Catalan nationalist parties emphasized instead the equality of citizenship implied in equality of access to the national language, and the collective right of Catalans to redress of the linguistic genocide attempted against them by the Franco regime. Concerned Catalan intellectuals supported this position, arguing that a bilingual policy was the path to linguistic substitution by Castilian and the eventual extinction of Catalan (Argenté *et al.* 1979). To the socialists' charge that any policy requiring the learning or use of Catalan would be no less an act of cultural imperialism than the imposition of Castilian on Catalans by the Franco regime, nationalists responded with a reminder that the Spanish Constitution and even the Catalan Statute of Autonomy privilege the language of the state.

   What is at issue here is not simply votes and seats in parliament, although these are not irrelevant. Both sides were attempting to balance a difficult equation whose terms are otherness and authenticity. The Catalan socialists sought to deny that there was any otherness at all ('one community that speaks two languages'), and ended by calling attention to difference. Their nationalist opponents began by calling attention to otherness and its historical sources in order to advocate its absorption and assimilation into what is authentically Catalan – an effort constantly undermined by the fact that all Catalans also speak Castilian. The alterity model is a difficult one to maintain because Catalans are so well acquainted with the language of the state, albeit by force rather than by choice.

Further complicating the question of linguistic normalization as national reconstruction was the fact that the integrity of the language was perceived to be threatened from within as well as from without. At this time in Catalonia's national life, a thoroughly internalized 'etiquette of accommodation' effectively limited the use of Catalan to conversations between native speakers, who would switch codes immediately in the presence of a Castilian speaker, or even an unknown interlocutor assumed to be a Castilian speaker (Woolard 1989, pp. 69–70).[2] There was rising concern that Castilian calques and lexical substitutions had been so normalized by two generations of use that they were now ineradicable; and that the unity of the language would succumb to the centrifugal force of its main dialectal variants (Eastern, Western, Valencian, and Balearic; see Fuster 1978, p. 117).

The Catalan parliament, elected in the spring of 1980, began drafting a language normalization law establishing the rights of Catalans to use their language for all official purposes, in education and in the media. The law was passed in April 1983, and it was preceded in 1982 by a public information campaign to sensitize people to the need for broad social acceptance and support of the new law. The pivot on which the campaign turned was a cartoon figure of a ten-year-old girl called 'Norma', whose name was a pun both on prescriptive syntax and orthography (*la norma*), and on the concept of normalization itself. Dressed in blue overalls and athletic shoes, holding her school notebook and proclaiming earnestly, 'Catalan is everyone's thing', she was conceived as a lively but nonthreatening, charmingly impertinent character who, being only ten years old, could say with impunity things that might sound rude or mocking if uttered by an adult (Direcció General de Política Lingüística 1983, pp. 14–16). She both exhorted and admonished, encouraging Castilian speakers to forget their inhibitions and start trying to speak Catalan, and correcting Catalan speakers who code-switched automatically to Castilian in the presence of anyone they thought they could identify as an 'immigrant', or who paid scant attention to the Castilianisms with which their own speech was littered.

By the early 1980s, then, the terms of public discourse about linguistic normalization were beginning to shift. Simply expanding the social space occupied by Catalan was no longer enough; language planners were now becoming equally concerned about *what kind* of Catalan people should be learning and speaking. Correct speech is not a new concern, or even one limited to modern life. The earliest known treatise on what Catalans call 'barbarisms' dates to 1487 (Solà 1977, p. 11). The meaning of correct speech has, however, changed from 'uncultivated' to inauthentic, from 'coarse words and rustic usages' (meaning, mainly, local forms of speech, especially rural ones, and dialectal variation) to the substitution of Castilian words for Catalan ones and, less obviously, the substitution of Castilian for Catalan syntax.

In 1986, a maverick socialist politician from Girona, Francesc Ferrer i Gironès, found in the experience of consumer society a particularly apt metaphor for what he saw happening to his nation. 'If "light" tobacco is without nicotine', he wrote (1986, p. 14), 'if "light" coffee is without caffeine, if "light" cola is without sugar, etc., then it is absolutely clear that "light" nationalism is nationalism without the nation.' This metaphor, a critique of his own party's temporizing on Spanish government policies adversely affecting Catalan autonomy, was almost instantly transferred to public discourse on language planning and linguistic authenticity. There is a considerable body of opinion favouring the acceptance of spoken Catalan, barbarisms and all, as the only valid standard against which to measure the written and formal spoken registers of Catalan. Some of the print and electronic media have already made this choice (see, for example, the *Llibre d'estil del Diari de Barcelona*, 1987), dismissing the Fabrian standard (the early twentieth century equivalent of 'light' Catalan) as a straitjacket that imprisons the language in stilted formalisms that constitute a barrier to access, not only for 'immigrants' but for native speakers as well. The nineteenth-century polemic of 'the Catalan we speak now' has been brought back to life (see Tubau 1990a), animated by a different range of meanings. Science as an authoritative discourse is being pressed to give way to what has been represented as the democratic power of the mass media, especially television (Tubau 1990b).

In this debate between the defenders of 'heavy' and 'light' Catalan, there is a most ingenious paradox at work. Those in favour of 'light' Catalan are generally located on the left wing of the political spectrum. Yet, in their eagerness to cast aside 'artificial' rules for correct usage, they have returned in a way to Prat de la Riba's notion of language as a natural phenomenon. They would, of course, be surprised to find themselves so closely allied with a historical figure that, for them, represents all that is politically and socially conservative, if not reactionary, in Catalan nationalist ideology (see DiGiacomo 1985, pp. 31–40).

Grounding the language debate: the teaching of Catalan

Formal instruction in Catalan, both for schoolchildren and for adults, is viewed by language planners as one of the principal means through which linguistic normalization will take place. Between February and June of 1987, as part of my research, I spent four mornings every week in a classroom at the Generalitat's Official Language School in Barcelona. There were 28 other adult students; all of us had taken a language competence examination, the results of which identified us as 'Catalan speakers', presumed to be at ease in casual conversation but unsure of the more formal and especially the written registers of the language.

Our course focused on the nuts and bolts of morphology and syntax at a level of abstraction that seemed to me more appropriate for a university-level course for future teachers of Catalan. We took the language to pieces, reading the brief literary excerpt at the beginning of each chapter of our text not for its aesthetic qualities, but only for its value in illustrating lexical, orthographic, syntactical and morphological problems. Similarly, we listened to literary passages read aloud in order to classify all the accent-bearing words into the correct category according to whether the accent fell on the last syllable, the penultimate syllable, or the pre-penultimate syllable (*paraules agudes, planes, o esdrúixoles*).

In short, the emphasis was on correctness most of the time, except when our attention was directed to the short section at the end of every chapter under the heading '*Què cal saber del català*' ('What you should know about Catalan'). These sections dealt with the history of the language; dialectal variation; the concept of 'standard' usage; degrees of formality and registers; in sum, with relativity and choice in the use of the language. The boundary between 'heavy' and 'light' models of linguistic authenticity was, on these occasions, revealed to be fluid and shifting in a way that made most of the class very uncomfortable. When was a 'barbarism' a matter of dialectal variation? How did you decide whether the use of non-standard forms connoted informality or ineptness?

What was at stake here for the students overlapped partially but not completely with what was at stake for our professor. All the students wanted, of course, to get a pass grade, but the sense of urgency had a variety of sources: pragmatic, ideological and personal. Some students had had their school fee paid for them by their employers and had been given time off from work to attend class; thus they felt themselves under pressure to justify this investment. Others were making a prospective investment in their own future, paying the fee out of their own pocket in the hope that their employment prospects would be brighter with proof of their ability to speak and write Catalan correctly. For some, both native and non-native Catalan speakers, taking the course was an index of the importance they attached to the connection between being Catalan and speaking Catalan, a step in the process of realizing an authentically Catalan identity. Most people had more than one reason. A young mother, concerned principally with being able to help her children with their Catalan homework, was also beginning to feel strongly enough about the identity question to speak Catalan at home, not only with her children but with her Castilian-speaking husband as well. The oldest student in the class, a 50-year-old woman from Lleida, in western Catalonia, found that being illiterate in her native language was an embarrassment both at work and in her personal life. Self-conscious about her *lleidatà* accent, she also wanted to speak the Catalan spoken in Barcelona; in many people's minds, rural usages and dialectal variation still add up to 'bad Catalan.' She was repeating the course, as was at least one other student who had failed it previously.

Our teacher, however, was engaged in a paradoxical endeavour, using his students' familiarity with Castilian to defamiliarize and eradicate from their speech Castilian calques and phonetics. This emphasis got him out of the discursive loop characteristic of much public discourse about Catalan usage, which focused mainly on lexical substitution and tended to harp on a few perennial 'barbarisms' (for example, *acera* [Cast.] for *vorera* [Cat.], 'sidewalk'). But choosing to fight the normalization battle on the grounds of phonological and syntactical accuracy also raised the stakes. It is harder to teach people to distinguish accurately and reliably between open and closed vowels, or between the voiced and voiceless 's' (neither distinction exists in Castilian), especially when actual usage varies widely. It is harder still to train people out of using Castilian calques that seem to come 'naturally' to them but result in scrambled Catalan syntax. Such constructions are an increasingly common feature of everyday speech (Sabater 1991, p. 101). For example, in Castilian the question ' ¿*Se lo dirás?*' – 'will you tell him/her/them?' – is often heard in Catalan as '*S'ho diràs?*' or '*Se'l diràs?*', ungrammatical because in Catalan the reflexive pronoun *se* never doubles, as it does in Castilian, as an indirect object pronoun.

Using another example, our teacher tried one day to defamiliarize Castilian by pointing out that the sentence '*Se lo pinta cada año*' had *four* possible translations in Catalan: '*s'ho pinta*' (he/she paints it [neuter gender] him/herself); '*se'l pinta*' (he/she paints it [masculine gender] him/herself); '*l'hi pinta*' (he/she paints it [masculine gender] for him/her); and '*li ho pinta*' (he/she paints it [neuter gender] for him/her). The point was to demonstrate that Castilian grammar can also be difficult, confusing, and improbable – a complaint students often voiced in class about Catalan grammar. The teacher's argument was met with disbelief; Castilian grammar was 'natural' and obvious, Catalan obscure and convoluted. When even native Catalan speakers appear to have learned to think in the syntactical structures of Castilian, the value and success of language teachers' and planners' efforts is placed in doubt, and the connection, whether scientifically or romantically constructed, between language, nation and identity appears threatened. As a professor of Catalan noted in a public lecture at the University of Barcelona, success also has its price, which can be calculated in the level of tension generated by issues of correctness and language choice in any speech event. He went so far as to suggest, only half in jest, that perhaps the trait that most distinguishes Catalonia from Spain is 'linguistic discomfort' (Larreula 1992).

The classroom exercises in which we were drilled added a further twist to the paradoxical relations of educational practice and language practice. All of these exercises were grounded in pedagogical techniques with which both professor and students were on intimately familiar terms, for they had all learned Castilian grammar in school. The exercise to which I referred earlier – the classification of accent-bearing words according to the syllable on which the accent fell – was strange only to me. Our teacher patiently explained the exercise and the categories to me a second time before we began, adding in response to my puzzled look, 'It's nothing revolutionary, you know'. He was right. Every student in the class had done this exercise in Castilian grammar classes, and so had most of their parents – just as they had also learned to classify Castilian verbs by conjugation, Castilian nouns according to the rules by which the plural is formed, and so on. The structure of the language-learning context is dominated by the pedagogical techniques through which Castilian grammar is taught.

The emphasis in such exercises is on lightning speed and accuracy, and there are many mistakes. Doubtless this is also the case in Castilian-language classrooms, but the consequences of such errors are, I would venture, significantly different. A poor performance in Castilian grammar would make a Spanish child a bad student, but not an inauthentic Spaniard. By contrast, in a Catalan classroom where students are comfortable with the (Castilian-style) pedagogy but not yet with the language, and in a society where language and identity are closely if problematically related, every wrong answer threatens more than a sense of competence and mastery.

The Catalan classroom is one of the arenas where social practice and language ideology collide, producing inconsistency and paradox. Castilian continues to 'occupy' the social space of the Catalan language class even as the instructor strives to eliminate its interference from the students' syntax and pronunciation (see Jaffe 1999 for an analysis of a related case, that of Corsican language instruction). The teaching of Catalan relies on the students' familiarity with both Castilian and the pedagogical strategies associated with it; the relative 'lightness' or 'heaviness' of Catalan usage takes its measure from Castilian. Both students and teachers of Catalan are confronted daily with the construct-edness of a national reality asserted – either in romantic or scientific terms – to be inscribed in the natural world.

Conclusions

This chapter has tried to steer clear of certain all-too-common errors in the study of nationalist social movements. Primordialist explanations are essentialist and ahistorical, assuming that activists' efforts to achieve cultural sovereignty constitute an attempt to defend and pre-serve a 'real' identity as opposed to the 'false' one imposed by the state (see, for example, Johnston 1991 for a neo-primordialist interpretation of Catalan nationalism). The heavy emphasis on 'tradition' suggests that nationalist movements are or should be a comparatively rare and relatively weak force in the modern world (for an example of this analysis applied to the Basque case; see Heiberg 1989) – an implausible argument given contemporary developments not only within European Union member states, but also in the former Yugoslavia and in the countries of the former Eastern bloc and Soviet Union.

Instrumentalist approaches, relying as they do on rational political/economic actor models of behaviour presumed to underlie all of social life, have great intuitive appeal but are misleading and limiting, reducing struggles over cultural sovereignty to the pursuit of political interests and economic advantage (see, for example, Hechter 1977), and leaving unanswered the question of how language came to be seen as a problem in need of regulation (Urla 1988, p. 382). Instrumentalism also presumes that economic and political power are coterminous, found together and in high concentration in the centre but thin on the peripheries of state systems. This, of course, leaves out of consideration such important cases as Catalonia, Euskadi and Scotland, all geographically 'peripheral' yet economically central.

The 'invention of tradition' approach proposed by Hobsbawm and Ranger (1983), to which this paper is conceptually indebted, is an explicit attempt to de-essentialize nationalist social movements and identities, to restore historical perspective and to explore the processes whereby traditions come to be self-evident realities and appeals to them acquire compelling force. However, the 'invented traditions' perspective on the nationalist movements of stateless nations has often been such that the 'imagined community' (Anderson 1983) comes to seem imaginary, 'constructed' meanings appear fabricated, and the putatively objective scholarly discourse of deconstruction verges on deauthorization (again, see Heiberg 1989 for an example of this type of analysis applied to the Basque case).

Even Hobsbawm himself seems lately inclined to this perspective. In the spring of 1992, the Catalan history journal *L'Avenç* published an interview with Hobsbawm by a Catalan historian, Xavier Marcet. Hobsbawm's central argument in *Nations and Nationalism Since 1870* is that, at the end of the twentieth century, nationalism was no longer either a progressive or even a viable political force in the world. This is a proposition that a Catalan historian is bound to challenge, and Marcet does, confronting Hobsbawm directly on the issue of whether nationalism falsifies history and pursuing this line of thought to ask why nationalism as an invented, constructed identity is so seldom examined as an attribute of the state (Marcet 1992, p. 27). 'Spanish nationalism' has an odd, unaccustomed sound. Indeed, to many Spanish political leaders, it is objectionable precisely because it suggests that Spanish identity has no greater claim to truth or reality than does Catalan identity, and for this very reason Catalans persist in using it.

When the conversation turns to language planning, Hobsbawm argues that a language-based national identity no longer makes sense in a world in which English has become the *lingua franca*, especially in the all-important technical and scientific fields: 'At present, it would be absurd to construct a vocabulary for molecular biology in Estonian' (Marcet 1992, p. 29). This assertion recalls one of Adolfo Suárez' first public statements following his appointment in 1976 as the head of the transitional government following Franco's death. Asked in an interview whether it was possible to use Catalan or Basque as a medium of upper-level instruction (*bachillerato*) in the schools, he replied, 'That's idiotic; first find me the professors who can teach nuclear chemistry in Basque, in Catalan. Let's be serious' (cited in Guardiola 1980, p. 90). The ensuing storm of protest eventually forced Suárez to apologize and retract the remark.

It is at the very least a most peculiar circumstance for a reformed fascist politician and a left-wing radical historian to find themselves on the same side of the same issue. I bring it up in order to point out that scholarly discourse is not, in fact, neutral. In historiography and ethnographic representation, as in politics, assertions of privileged detachment are likely to be read by Catalans as an implicit defence of hegemonic forces and their dominating power.

Where does this leave the ethnographic study of language ideology and language planning as central aspects of many nationalist social movements? In this chapter I have made extensive use of the notion that identities are not given, but constructed and reinvented through historical processes, arguing that although nationalist ideology asserts and stresses continuity, social experience reflects changing subjectivity. The Catalan case nicely illustrates one such shift in how people understand their everyday experience: that which recast nineteenth-century romantic ideas about the relation between language and nation in the modern idiom of science. Through the scientific study of language and the design and implementation of new language policies, Catalan political leaders have, like their Basque counterparts, turned the ideological tools of the state to their own purposes in order to resist Spanish control over the mechanisms of cultural reproduction.

Both the romantic and the scientific mode of envisioning the relation between language and nation are, however, open to challenge from within as well as from without. The identities they strive to protect from state power are not primordial or essential, but emergent in the process of resistance (Urla 1988, p. 391). The past is invoked and given concrete present reality in fragmentary form, as the nineteenth-century debate over '*el català que ara es parla*' shows. When science absorbed and transformed this debate in the twentieth century, Catalan language planners found their task not only facilitated but complicated by the discourse and strategies of cultural reproduction they had appropriated from the state. Theories of developmental psychology and census data defining linguistic populations lent plausibility not only to their arguments, but to those of their critics. Catalan socialists, appealing to the immigrant vote at home and their political allies in Madrid, called upon these same data and theories in defence of the right of Castilian-speaking children to be educated in their 'maternal language' (Mata 1980) – the same right that was denied to Catalan children and their parents under the Franco regime. Native speakers of Balearic, Valencian, or western Catalan feel increasingly resentful of what they perceive as a new form of cultural imperialism emanating not from Madrid, but from Barcelona, where standard Catalan is defined. And adult students of Catalan, whether native or non-native speakers, feel caught between competing models of linguistic authenticity.

The constructed and emergent nature of a Catalan identity rooted in language is, then, made daily apparent to Catalans, but from this very few people draw the conclusion that teaching science, publishing newspapers, or conducting the business of government in Catalan is 'absurd'. Instead, this peculiar and in certain ways privileged angle of vision tends to dissolve the taken-for-grantedness of the state and its attributes, exposing *their* constructedness. Catalans habitually refer to the language we are accustomed to call 'Spanish' as Castilian, stressing its regional origin and refusing to conflate it with the state, which is likewise seldom referred to as Spain, but more typically as 'the Spanish state', a formulation that suggests man-made political institutions rather than a nation in the romantic sense.

At a time when the European Union is remaking the political lives of its constituent states, Catalans have seized the opportunities it offers stateless nations to become visible on the world stage (see DiGiacomo 1999). This is not mere opportunism. Catalans believe they have a role to play *as Catalans* in the construction of a new and more egalitarian Europe. The philologist Isidor Marí has argued recently (1996, p. 80) that 'the construction of European economic, political and cultural unity will be neither possible nor desirable if it is understood as a process leading to forced uniformity'. His point of departure, ironically enough, is a story told by François Mitterand, whose view of the dangers of 'linguistic rivalry' was well known (see Pujol 1995, p. 9), to illustrate the spirit in which the construction of the new Europe should be undertaken. During the Middle Ages, a pilgrim came upon two workmen, and paused to ask what they were doing. One answered that he was putting up a wall; the other replied, 'I am building a cathedral'. Continuing the metaphor, Marí rejects the overworked image of the Tower of Babel (1996, p. 81):

> reality is by nature – fortunately – multilingual, and the safeguard-ing of linguistic and cultural pluralism, like all other forms of demo-cratic pluralism, cannot be viewed as a punishment, but as one of the noblest enterprises to which we can dedicate our efforts. Learning and teaching languages is also a way of advancing in this

direction, unless we set ourselves to building invisible walls instead of a cathedral for all Europeans.

Catalan national character is widely believed – in Spain as well as in Catalonia – to possess an enhanced capacity for irony. Catalan intellectuals point to Josep Pla, a literary figure whose ironic vision is legendary. A Spanish journalist (Ochoa 1992), writing about the value of irony, notes its tendency to flourish on the peripheries of the state that lie farthest from the centre – Catalonia and Galicia – where geographic distance produces aesthetic distance from both other and self, building ironies upon ironies.

Stereotypes of national character aside, the Catalan experience evidences a good deal of dissonance and ambiguity, the raw materials of irony. Neither the calculating rationalism of instrumentalist theories nor the idealism of primordialist approaches can do justice to the ironic condition of stateless nations in the modern world; and interpreting them out of existence, as Hobsbawm lately seems inclined to do, is simply to take the state's part against them. Ethnographic accounts of nationalist social movements should be sensitive to the play of ironies rather than attempting to reduce them to certainties of questionable explanatory value.

Notes

1. All translations in this chapter are my own.
2. Catalan was and remains a high-prestige language, associated with middle-class status, educational achievement and professional employment, but in 1980 its social value was variable, depending on who spoke it to whom. As Woolard discovered (1984, p. 70; 1989, pp. 122–3), the most positive personal and social characteristics were attributed to native speakers of both Catalan and Castilian using their native language. Native Castilian speakers reacted quite negatively to second-language Catalan speakers, while Catalans regarded them with relative indifference. In order to use the language for social advancement, then, native Castilian speakers who learned Catalan had to be so proficient that they could 'pass' as native Catalan speakers.

   This picture had changed by 1987 (see Woolard 1990). Six years of language planning and policy by the Generalitat had sufficiently altered the linguistic environment that the link between language choice and ascribed ethnic identity had been significantly loosened, and the line separating native and non-native speech had been blurred, though not erased, as the debate on 'light' versus 'heavy' Catalan shows. In short, Catalan had in fact been 'normalized' in important ways. However, although the social consequences of language choice had ceased to conflict with the status considerations motivating Castilian speakers to adopt Catalan, the continuing *de facto* linguistic segregation of neighbourhoods and workplaces posed – and still poses – an obstacle to the informal acquisition of Catalan through everyday interaction with Catalan speakers.

Bibliography

Amelang, J.S. *Honored Citizens of Barcelona: Patrician Culture and Class Relations, 1490–1714* (Princeton, New Jersey: Princeton University Press, 1986).

Anderson, B. *Imagined Communities: Reflections on the Origin and Spread of Nationalism* (London: Verso Editions and NLB, 1983).

Ardit, M., Balcells, A. and Sales, N. *Història dels Països Catalans. De 1714 a 1975* (Barcelona: EDHASA, 1980).

Argenté, J., *et al.* 'Una nació sense estat, un poble sense llengua?', *Els Marges*, 15 (1979) 3–13.

Benet, J. *Catalunya sota el règim franquista* (Barcelona: Editorial Blume, 1978).

Candel, F. *Los otros catalanes* (Barcelona: Ediciones Península, 1964).

Castellet, J.M. and Molas, J. eds *Antologia general de la poesia catalana* (Barcelona: Edicions 62 i 'la Caixa', 1979).

Cervantes Saavedra, M. *Don Quixote*. J.M. Cohen, trans. (Baltimore, Maryland: Penguin Books, 1950).

Comelles, J.M. (S.M. DiGiacomo, trans.) 'Psychiatric Care in Relation to the Development of the Contemporary State: the Case of Catalonia', *Culture, Medicine and Psychiatry*, 15 (1991) 193–215.

DiGiacomo, S.M. *The Politics of Identity: Nationalism in Catalonia* (Ann Arbor, Michigan: University Microfilms International, 1985).

DiGiacomo, S.M. 'Images of Class and Ethnicity in Catalan Politics, 1977–1980', in G.W. McDonogh, ed., *Conflict in Catalonia: Images of an Urban Society* (Gainesville, FL: University of Florida Monographs in Social Sciences, Number 71, University of Florida Press, 1986), pp. 72–92.

DiGiacomo, S.M. 'Language Ideological Debates in an Olympic City: Barcelona, 1992–1996', in J. Blommaert, ed., *Language Ideological Debates:* (Berlin: Mouton de Gruyter, 1999), pp. 105–42.

Direcció General de Política Lingüística *La campanya per la normalització lingüística de Catalunya 1982* (Barcelona: Departament de Cultura de la Generalitat de Catalunya, 1983).

Duarte, C. and Massip, A. *Síntesi d'història de la llengua catalana* (Barcelona: La Magrana, 1981).

Elliott, J.H. *The Revolt of the Catalans: a Study in the Decline of Spain 1598–1640* (Cambridge: Cambridge University Press, 1963).

Fabra, P. *La llengua catalana i la seva normalització* (Barcelona: Edicions 62 i 'la Caixa', 1980).

Fàbregas, X. 'Una polèmica que cal agafar amb pinces', *L'Avenç*, 27 (1980) 43–6.

Ferrando, A. and Nicolás, M. *Panorama d'història de la llengua* (València: Tàndem Edicions, 1993).

Ferrer i Gironès, F. *La persecució de la llengua catalana* (Barcelona: Edicions 62, 1985).

Ferrer i Gironès, F. *Catalunya light ...? Els espanyols no són catalans* (Barcelona: El Llamp, 1986).

Foucault, M. 'The Subject and Power', in P. Rabinow and H. Dreyfus, *Michel Foucault: Beyond Structuralism and Hermeneutics* (Chicago: University of Chicago Press, 1982) pp. 208–26.

Fuster, J. *El Congrés de Cultura Catalana* (Barcelona: Laia, 1978).

Galí, A. *Història de les institucions i del moviment cultural a Catalunya, 1900–1936. Llibre I, La llengua: entitats defensores i propagadores* (Barcelona: Fundació Alexandre Galí, 1979).

Guardiola, C.-J. *Per la llengua. Llengua i cultura als Països Catalans, 1939–1977* (Barcelona: La Magrana, 1980).

Hechter, M. *Internal Colonialism: the Celtic Fringe in British National Development, 1536–1966* (London: Routledge and Kegan Paul, 1975).

Heiberg, M. *The Making of the Basque Nation* (New York: Cambridge University Press, 1989).

Hobsbawm, E., and Ranger, T. eds *The Invention of Tradition* (New York: Cambridge University Press, 1983).

Jaffe, A. *Ideologies in Action: Language Politics on Corsica* (New York: Mouton de Gruyter, 1999).

Johnston, H. *Tales of Nationalism: Catalonia, 1939–1979* (New Brunswick, New Jersey: Rutgers University Press, 1991).

Larreula i Vidal, E. Public lecture on cultural obstacles to the normalization of Catalan in schools and universities. *Jornades Sobre Llengua i Ensenyament*, University of Barcelona, September 9, 1992.

Lass, A. 'Romantic Documents and Political Monuments: the Meaning-Fulfillment of History in 19th-Century Czech Nationalism', *American Ethnologist*, 15 (1988) 456–71.

Llibre d'estil del Diari de Barcelona Un model de llengua pels mitjans de comunicació (Barcelona: Editorial Empúries, 1987).

López del Castillo, Ll. *El català a través del temps* (Barcelona: Nova Terra, 1987).

Marcet i Gisbert, X. 'Conversa amb Eric J. Hobsbawm', *L'Avenç*, 158 (1992) 24–9.

Marí, I. *Plurilingüisme europeu i llengua catalana* (València: Universitat de València, 1996).

Mata i Garriga, M. PSC-PSOE Party Position on Education, in *Immigració i reconstrucció nacional a Catalunya* (Barcelona: Publicacions de la Fundació Jaume Bofill and Editorial Blume, 1980) pp. 137–45.

McDonogh, G.W. *Good Families of Barcelona: a Social History of Power in the Industrial Era* (Princeton, New Jersey: Princeton University Press, 1986).

Ochoa, E. 'Oblícuamente concava', *El País Semanal*, no. 80, p. 84, August 30 (1992).

Prat de la Riba, E. *La nacionalitat catalana*. Barcelona: Edicions 62 i 'la Caixa', 1978 (1906).

Pujol, J. *Què representa la llengua a Catalunya?* (Barcelona: Generalitat de Catalunya, 1995).

Recolons i Arquer, Ll. 'El marc demogràfic dels recents moviments migratoris de Catalunya', *Perspectiva Social*, 14 (1979) 7–34.

Sahlins, P. *Boundaries: the Making of France and Spain in the Pyrenees* (Berkeley: University of California Press, 1989).

Sahlins, P. 'State Formation and National Identity in the Catalan Borderlands during the Eighteenth and Nineteenth Centuries', in T.M. Wilson and H. Donnan, eds, *Border Identities: Nation and State at International Frontiers* (New York: Cambridge University Press, 1998), pp. 31–61.

Solà, J. *Del català incorrecte al català correcte. Història dels criteris de correcció lingüística* (Barcelona: Edicions 62, 1977).

Solà, J. 'El català que ara es parla', *L'Avenç*, 27 (1980) 47–54.

Tubau, I. *El català que ara es parla. Llengua i periodisme a la ràdio i la televisió* (Barcelona: Empúries, 1990a).

Tubau, I. *Paraula viva contra llengua normativa* (Barcelona: Editorial Laertes, 1990b).

Urla, J. 'Ethnic Protest and Social Planning: a Look at Basque Language Revival', *Cultural Anthropology*, 3 (1988) 379–94.

Urla, J. 'Cultural Politics in an Age of Statistics: Numbers, Nations, and the Making of Basque Identity', *American Ethnologist*, 20 (1993) 818–43.

Vallverdú, F. *Dues llengues, dues funcions?* 2nd edn (Barcelona: Edicions 62, 1979).

Woolard, K.A. 'A Formal Measure of Language Attitudes in Barcelona: a Note from Work in Progress', *International Journal of the Sociology of Language*, 47 (1984), 63–71.

Woolard, K.A. *Double Talk: Bilingualism and the Politics of Ethnicity in Catalonia* (Stanford, California: Stanford University Press, 1989).

Woolard, K.A., and Tae-Joong Gahng 'Changing Language Policies and Attitudes in Autonomous Catalonia', *Language in Society*, 19 (1990), 311–30.

Yxart, J. *Entorn de la literatura catalana de la restauració.* J. Castellanos, ed. (Barcelona: Edicions 62 i 'la Caixa', 1980).

5
Irish Language, Irish Identity: Northern Ireland and the Republic of Ireland in the European Union

Camille C. O'Reilly

Introduction

The Irish language has been an important issue in Ireland for centuries, although in differing ways during different periods. Once the sole primary language of communication, since the Anglo-Norman invasion of 1169, Irish has been at odds with the language of invaders. Still, Irish remained the primary means of communication for almost every group and class up until the seventeenth century. After the defeat at the Battle of Kinsale in 1601, however, Ireland lost much of its Irish-speaking nobility and the fortunes of the language began to change (Ó Donnaile 1997). Perceived as a threat by the various ruling groups from that period on, efforts were made to establish English as the language of law, government and the social elite. Sometimes through legislation, like the infamous Statutes of Kilkenny, but more often through social and economic pressure and oppression, the Irish language experienced a period of long, gradual decline.[1]

English-speakers came to dominate in positions of power, first militarily, then politically and economically and, finally, socially. By 1800, no one seeking to improve or even maintain their social or economic position in society could do so without the English language (Ó Donnaile 1997, p. 196). Irish speakers were politically and economically marginalized, and the Irish language was in danger of giving way entirely to English. The final stages of this linguistic shift happened during the nineteenth century, when English came to be viewed by the majority of people as the natural and essential medium of Irish society in all spheres of life. However, with Irish safely confined to the periphery and English secure in its dominant position, the time was ripe for the Celtic revival.

The revival was not limited to Ireland – a fascination with things Celtic swept Europe in the wake of the Ossian forgeries of the 1760s, and was further fuelled by the growing influence of Romantic philosophy. This – combined with the relatively secure position of English in Ireland and Ireland in the United Kingdom – made possible the first phase of interest in the revival and survival of the Irish language. Interest in the language at this time was almost entirely antiquarian. The first revival movement of the late eighteenth to early nineteenth century, and the second, which took place in the 1830s and 40s, were both focused on scholarly research into the history of Ireland and the Irish language.

Crowley highlights the importance of this appeal to the ancient history of Irish for the validation of Irish language and culture. From the second half of the nineteenth century onwards, it formed the basis of a call for Irish unity and claims of cultural and national difference from Britain (Crowley 1996, pp. 107–8). The irony is that even as antiquarians and Celtic enthusiasts sang the praises of the Irish language and argued for its revival, many native speakers felt ashamed of their language and worked to acquire English to ensure their economic survival.

In spite of the influence of Romanticism, the Irish language has not always been associated with the struggle for political independence. Although some clearly connected the Irish language to claims for the uniqueness of the Irish people, there was certainly no straightforward association with nationalism up to the middle of the nineteenth century. One of the heroes of Irish nationalism from that period was Daniel O'Connell, a native speaker of Irish who carried out his political agenda primarily through the English language and who once said he could 'witness without a sigh the gradual disuse of the Irish' (Crowley 1996, p. 111). The famine of 1845–49 dramatically reduced the population of Irish speakers, who because of their location in western and poorer regions were disproportionately affected by death and immigration (Ó Riagáin 1997, pp. 4–5). As the situation of the Irish language grew more precarious, its supporters became more vocal and calls for its restoration become more strident.

The third Irish language revival spans the period from the 1880s to the founding of the Irish Free State in 1921. This phase of the movement was spearheaded by the Gaelic League, an organization which was founded in 1895 and led by Douglas Hyde until 1915. It was during this period that an association between the Irish language and Irish cultural and political nationalism crystallized. The philosophies of

Herder, Schlegel and Fichte were extremely influential in the development of nineteenth-century cultural nationalism throughout Europe, and Ireland is no exception. Fichte wrote that 'it is beyond doubt that, wherever a separate language is found, there a separate nation exists, which has the right to take charge of its independent affairs and to govern itself' (1968, p. 184). This belief underpins the ideology of cultural nationalism, making the Irish language one of the key justifications in calls for Irish independence, necessitating the language's survival and revival. It is epitomized by one slogan of the era, '*gan teanga, gan tír*' – no language, no country. By the time the Irish Free State was established in 1921, the Irish language had become a key symbol of the nation, encapsulating many of the ideals espoused by cultural and political nationalists alike.

Efforts to revive the Irish language continued both north and south of the border after partition in 1921. The socio-political context in which the revival was situated differed dramatically, however, which led to a divergence in strategies and, over time, in interpretations of the significance and symbolic meaning of the language. The way Irish identity is constructed gradually diverged as well, as did the position of the language in those constructions. The relationship between identity and the Irish language grows from same historical roots – and in some instances is linked to the same ideologies – both north and south of the border, but it has developed along different trajectories postpartition.

The Republic of Ireland: old language, new state, new meanings

In the immediate aftermath of partition, *Gaeilgeoirí* (Irish speakers and activists) in the North had to come to terms with the new Unionist administration. In the South, meanwhile, many goals of the Irish language revival movement became policy for the new government of the Free State. Irish became the 'national' language (with English recognized as an official language), and remains so to this day. In spite of the severe decline of the language, its existence was a key plank in the nationalist justification for an independent state.

According to Ó Riagáin (1997), the language strategy of the Irish state in the 1920s and 1930s had four elements. First was the maintenance of Irish in areas where it was still the community language (the *Gaeltacht*). Though containing just 16 per cent of the population, the Irish-speaking areas were the most impoverished, so this element took on many aspects of a development programme. The second element was a revival strategy for the rest of the country where the population was almost entirely English speaking. In practice, this focused on the educational system as a means of increasing the number of Irish speakers in the population. The third element was to introduce the use of Irish into the public service, while the fourth was to modernize and standardize the language (Ó Riagáin 1997, p. 15).

Language policy in the Republic of Ireland has gone through three phases. From 1922 to 1948, the developing language policy focused on the four elements identified above – the *Gaeltacht*, education, public administration and standardization (Ó Riagáin 1997). This was the most optimistic phase, but one in which policy was based on nationalist ideals and ideology with very little concrete evidence or research to point the way forward. Ó Riagáin labels the middle phase, from 1948 to 1970, 'stagnation and retreat' (1997, p. 19). Popular support of government language policies had long since declined, and political commitment to the revival weakened significantly. During this period there began a shift in focus in the revival movement from state action on its own towards sustainable public support. The third phase of 'benign neglect' spans the three decades from 1970 to the present day.[2] Since the 1970s there have been significant changes in the social and economic organization of Irish society and these have influenced language policy. The impact of relative economic prosperity and increasing cultural influence from outside the country is complex, but one consequence has been difficulties in implementing policies meant to maintain Irish as a minority language. During this period policies have been realigned to emphasize language maintenance, with a weakening of policies aimed at language revival.

There has only been an organized effort to gauge public attitudes towards the Irish language and language policies since the establishment of the Committee on Irish Language Attitudes Research (CILAR) in 1970. CILAR conducted a national survey in 1973, and two more were conducted by the *Institiúid Teangeolaíochta Éireann* (ITÉ) in 1983 and 1993. The surveys can be grouped according to three main theoretical perspectives, the ethnicity/ethnolinguistic vitality perspective, language as capital and language policy. The results are complex,[3] but a few significant conclusions can be made in each of these three areas.

All three show a fairly consistent association between the language and Irish ethnic identity, although, significantly, this does not appear to correlate with language use. Even those respondents who held the most positive attitudes towards the language as an element of their identity were pessimistic about its future survival. In terms of capital, there is a consistent 20 to 30 per cent minority across all three surveys who value the Irish language for its own sake. However, the economic value attached to Irish is very low compared to English, and has declined since the compulsory nature of Irish language education was eased after 1973.[4] In terms of policy, public support is low for those policies which impinge directly on the lives of individuals. In contrast, there is a substantial majority who favour government support for language organizations, having the language taught in the schools in a non-compulsory fashion, and for government officials who conduct their business through Irish (all of the above from Ó Riagáin 1997, Chapter 6).

While the situation of Irish today is not particularly encouraging, it is still not as dire as many had predicted it would be by the end of the twentieth century. Although shrinking, there are still *Gaeltachtaí* in the South containing roughly 2 per cent of the population. One area in which Irish is experiencing a small but significant growth is Irish-medium education. A policy of 'Gaelicizing' education was put in place by the southern government in the 1920s. Schools were encouraged to introduce immersion programmes where all or part of the school curriculum was taught through the medium of Irish. At its highest point in the 1950s, just over half of state primary schools offered full or partial immersion programmes (Ó Riagáin 1997, pp. 20–1). The policy proved unpopular with parents, however, and numbers declined throughout the 1960s and 1970s. From a high of 255 Irish medium schools outside of *Gaeltacht* areas in 1940/41, numbers sank to 24 in 1970/71. Interest in Irish-medium education has grown again in recent years, with the result that by 1990/91 there were 66 all-Irish schools in the Republic. That number rose to 80 in 1994 (Ó Riagáin 1997, p. 201). The recent growth in the number of Irish-medium schools is especially significant because it is parent-led, in contrast to the government-sponsored initiatives of the past.

As indicated by the surveys over the last three decades, many people in the South have ambiguous feelings about the Irish language. There has been an increasing antipathy towards Irish nationalism during this period as well, with serious questions raised by the violence in Northern Ireland and by the work of revisionist historians, fuelling debates in the popular media about a changing Irish identity. Hindley (1990, p. 163), among others, has suggested that nationalist sentiment is important to the survival of Irish in an overwhelmingly English-speaking country. This is probably true, but it is also problematic in light of the antagonism shown towards Irish nationalism by so many Irish people.

Northern Ireland: revival and opposition

There is no consensus in either the Republic of Ireland or Northern Ireland about the meaning and significance of the language, beyond a general sense of its symbolic importance. The debate, however, takes place in a very different context north and south of the border. After partition, Northern Ireland remained a part of the United Kingdom, but was ruled from a separate parliament at Stormont. The British and Unionist ethos of the state is clearly expressed by the slogan 'a Protestant state for a Protestant people'. Although Catholics with an Irish identity made up approximately one-third of the population, they were largely excluded from positions of power and influence politically, economically and socially.[5]

In a society which is fundamentally divided on political grounds, to learn or to speak Irish is perceived as an act which has political implications. Those who choose to do so inevitably have had to define their own sense of how the language relates to their political identity. The great majority of people who relate positively to the Irish language in Northern Ireland are Catholic and nationalist, having an Irish rather than a British sense of identity. While some Protestants have taken an interest in the language, its relationship to their identity is somewhat problematic and differs significantly from that of Catholics. For this reason, when talking about the Irish language and identity in Northern Ireland I am referring only to the Catholic/nationalist population.[6]

While the current resurgence of interest in Irish is perhaps the most vibrant it has been in a century, the Irish language is not new to the North. Revival activities have gone on sporadically in what is now Northern Ireland for two centuries, as elsewhere on the island. In the eighteenth century, Belfast was an important centre for Irish-language activities. The Linenhall Library started a collection of books and manuscripts in Irish, the Harpers' Festival was held in the city, and Irish was first taught in the Belfast Academy towards the end of that century. The first printed periodical in Irish, *Bolg an tSolair*, was started in Belfast in 1795. Up to the beginning of the nineteenth century, Irish was still widely spoken in isolated pockets of Counties Antrim and Down. Revival activities continued in the North throughout the nineteenth and early twentieth centuries, with surges of interest at the turn of the century and again in the 1950s.

For the 50-year period from partition to 1972, the Ulster Unionist Party ruled Northern Ireland's parliament. The dominant ideological forces of Northern Irish society under this regime were inimical to the Irish language, and the state itself was self-consciously anti-Irish (Andrews 1997; Mac Póilin 1995, p. 10). Official policy reflected the attitude that Irish was a foreign language with no place in Northern Ireland. For example, Irish was banned from BBC Northern Ireland for 50 years, even though Scots Gaelic and Welsh programmes had been broadcast by the BBC in Scotland and Wales respectively since the 1920s (Andrews 1992, pp. 25–57; Cathcart 1984). In the schools, a sustained effort was made for three decades to undermine the position of Irish in the education system. Today, Irish is treated like other modern languages such as German and French, but attempts have been made to undermine even this limited status.

Because the main focus of revival efforts in the North has been in the schools, an overall picture of the status of Irish in Northern Ireland is perhaps best obtained by examining educational policy over the past century. In 1904, Irish was recognized for the first time as a medium of schooling in areas where the majority of children spoke Irish as their home language. While this measure came into effect for the whole of Ireland, by this time there were very few areas left in the six counties which were to become Northern Ireland where a significant number of children spoke the language. Although the position of Irish in the educational system of Northern Ireland remained relatively unchanged after partition, from that point on any new regulations which were introduced were restrictive rather than encouraging.

Throughout the 1920s, efforts to improve the status of Irish in the schools were met with stalwart opposition. For example, during the mid-1920s, *Comhaltas Uladh*, the northern branch of the Gaelic League, lobbied the British Ministry of Education for a more flexible attitude towards Irish. While *Comhaltas Uladh* sought to introduce Irish to classes below the third grade, in 1926, the Ministry of Education actually restricted it further to grades five, six and seven. In 1933, all special grants for the teaching of Irish were terminated. At the time about 10 500 children were learning Irish in primary school, 14.11 per cent of children at Catholic schools, 5 per cent of the total primary population (Maguire 1991, p. 43).

Throughout the history of Northern Ireland, government policy has continued to oscillate between hostility and disregard, although more enlightened attitudes have been demonstrated on occasion since the fall of Stormont. For example, in 1974 the Department of Education issued a report which advocated second language teaching in general, and which acknowledged the particular attributes of Irish (Maguire 1991, p. 74). Unfortunately, none of this was reinforced in any concrete way through policy or planning initiatives.

In spite of official attitudes of indifference and antipathy, the Irish language has continued to find a niche in the North, and interest has been growing at a steady rate since the early 1980s. Classes are organized wherever there is a group of interested people. Over the past two decades the Irish-medium schools have been the heart of the revival movement in Northern Ireland. The first all-Irish primary school, *Bunscoil Phobal Feirste*, was established in Belfast in 1971 to cater for the children of the Shaws Road *Gaeltacht*.[7] Since then, five other primary schools have opened in Belfast alone, and another six in other parts of the North. All of the Irish-medium schools were established without government support, relying on the donations of parents and the local people for funding. *Bunscoil Phobal Feirste* operated for 13 years without government recognition, and the second school, *Gaelscoil na bhFál*, for six. The other schools have pursued a variety of strategies to obtain government funding, but all have had to operate without funding for years at a time. One of the newer schools in Belfast, *Bunscoil an Droichead*, which opened in 1996, was the first to start up with European funding.[8] There are now two other schools receiving European funds, one in County Antrim and the other in County Derry. As the number of Irish-medium primary schools has grown, a number of secondary schools have been established.[9] There are also numerous Irish-medium nursery schools (*naoínraí*) which are preparing increasingly large numbers of children for entry into the primary schools.[10]

In addition to the teaching of the language to adults and the establishment of Irish-medium schools, there is a great deal of language revival activity in Belfast. The Irish language newspaper *Lá* is based in the city and distributed throughout Ireland. There is an Irish language cultural centre in west Belfast, *An Cultúrlann McAdam – O Fiaich*, which houses a bilingual cafe, Irish language bookstore, theatre and drama group, and is the venue for cultural events through Irish. Belfast's Shaws Road (see above) houses the only urban neo-*Gaeltacht* in Ireland. The development of business and employment opportunities for Irish speakers has become a key focus of the revival in recent years, particularly as growing numbers of young people leave Irish-medium education. Belfast has an Irish language business development agency called *Forbairt Feirste* which offers classes through the medium of Irish and supports the establishment of businesses which operate primarily through Irish.

Irish has become an important aspect of national identity for nationalists in the North whether or not they can actually speak the language. In fact, the Irish language has become one of the few issues which can unite the majority of nationalists of all political descriptions. A number of different campaigns have mustered fairly widespread support, including the putting up of Irish street signs and, especially, Irish-medium education. It is not all unity and agreement, of course. Individuals and groups with different interests compete to have their version of the meaning and significance of the Irish language accepted, with consequences for the shape of Irish identity and for power relations at all levels in Northern Irish society.

As ethnographers such as Handler (1988) and McDonald (1989) have highlighted, language and ethnicity can be constructed as part of an oppositional identity. This is conceptualized through different versions of history, language and tradition, including both versions that contest dominant ideological constructions and those that compete with other oppositional constructions. The appropriation of history, or the assertion of alternative histories, is an important means of challenging or subverting dominant discourses, while the links between history and language provide new opportunities to reinvent identity. In Northern Ireland, competing versions of the significance of Irish, both within the nationalist community and between nationalists and government institutions, are part of an ideological struggle to define Irish identity, and to have this identity officially recognized.

The Irish language has become an alternative point of political access for many nationalists. It provides a means of accumulating political, symbolic and cultural capital both within the nationalist community and in the wider political milieu. In the context of political strife and the historical repression of Irish identity in the North, the Irish language offers an opportunity for people to assert their sense of Irishness. For many, it is also a chance to make a compelling but non-violent statement about being Irish in a situation where opportunities to do so have been severely limited by prejudice and violence. For those whose access to economic, educational and social resources has been limited, Irish can offer fresh opportunities.

As such, Irish has become an important tool of political organization in Northern Ireland. In an 'abnormal' political situation, the Irish language revival movement has become a meaningful mode of political expression and participation. There are a number of reasons why this is so. The history of inequality and lack of political representation for the Catholic minority in the North has left its legacy, and even though much has been done to address Catholic grievances, inequality still exists. The violence and civil unrest that have characterized most of the history of Northern Ireland, especially during the last 30 years, have severely limited possibilities for political participation for most people. The political structures that do exist offer few opportunities for participation or expression and very little real power for either Catholics or Protestants. And finally, the dominant British ethos of the state continues to stifle political and cultural expressions of Irishness, even with the limited progress made in recent years as a result of new policies intended to nurture the 'two traditions', and rhetoric about 'parity of esteem'.[11] The new institutions put in place during the peace process of the last few years are designed in part to deal with these problems but it remains to be seen how effective they will be.

The Irish language movement has become an important avenue for demands that an Irish political and cultural identity be recognized by the state. As an Irish identity becomes increasingly legitimate in Northern Ireland, the question becomes which version – or versions – of this identity will dominate and who will control or influence its shape. Funding and other forms of official recognition can be used to manipulate this process. Ideologies can be promoted through the adoption of certain discourses by institutions of power or delegitimized through strategies such as the 'depoliticization' of the Irish language.

The Irish language in the North has become for many a symbol and tool of resistance not just for the goals and ideals of republicanism, but in the context of a new politics of culture and ethnicity. The Irish language was promoted by both Sinn Féin and the SDLP during the peace negotiations as part of a package for official recognition of an Irish identity in the North. Both parties continue to link recognition for the Irish language with parity of esteem, as does the Dublin government. During the all-party talks in Castle Buildings at Stormont in 1998 and 1999, some members of Sinn Féin, the SDLP and representatives of the southern government conversed in Irish in the halls and over lunch. Although at an unofficial level, Irish was spoken at the talks on a daily basis between those people who were fluent in the language. Concessions made to the Catholic community in Northern Ireland as part of the political process include increased support for the

Irish language, particularly in respect of Irish-medium schools.[12] All of these things have contributed to the association of Irish with a Catholic/nationalist cultural package. This will have consequences for Protestants interested in the language, as the discourse of 'two traditions' comes to dominate that of 'common heritage', and the Irish language returns to a solid position in the Nationalist cultural and political repertoire.

Irish language, Irish identity

I have argued elsewhere that the complexities and intricacies of the Irish language revival can be understood through an examination of the discourses of the movement (O'Reilly 1999). I see discourse as a lin-guistic vehicle for thought, communication and ideology; its use and creation an action that involves the exercise of power. As part of our experience of social reality, ideology is constituted through discourse – it is expressed, reproduced and changed through discourse. At the same time, the frameworks which shape discourse are themselves formed with reference to existing ideologies. Meaning can be invested and reinvested into different discourses, varying according to context. The discourses used *in* the Irish language revival movement and to talk *about* the Irish language are both similar and different north and south of the border. A comparison of these similarities and differences reveals much about shifting notions of Irish identity in relation to the lan-guage, and its changing position vis-à-vis the United Kingdom and the European Union.

Talk by nationalists about the Irish language in Northern Ireland can be divided into three separate discourses, while in the Republic there are four. While this breakdown does not exhaust all the possibilities, it covers the most important ideological streams of debate within the revival movement. I have called the Northern discourses decolonizing discourse, cultural discourse (north), and rights discourse. The three parallel discourses in the Republic are national language discourse, cul-tural discourse (south), and minority language discourse, with the fourth being dead language discourse The descriptions which follow are of necessity only brief sketches, meant to give a feel for the dis-courses and their related ideologies in Northern Ireland and the Republic.[13]

Decolonizing discourse and national language discourse share the same roots, although they have developed in quite different directions since partition. Along with cultural discourse, these discourses have a relatively long history. During the first part of the twentieth century, the Gaelic League split over ideological disagreements about the strong association some were making between the Irish language and the political independence of Ireland, ultimately leading to the resignation of Douglas Hyde from his position as president in 1915. From its inception, the Gaelic League had two separate and sometimes contradictory emphases – the cultural independence and the political independence of Ireland. Decolonizing discourse in Northern Ireland has developed primarily from the political independence strain of Gaelic League thought, although still incorporating an idea of cultural independence.

Over time, national language discourse has come to draw more heavily from the cultural independence strain. Since the Republic achieved its political independence, the priority has shifted towards the development and definition of a unique Irish identity and culture. However, there is still a perception among a substantial minority of the population that the Irish language makes Ireland more independent of England. This assertion was supported by between 37 and 41 per cent of respondents in each of the three language attitudes surveys conducted from 1973 to 1993 (Ó Riagáin and Ó Gliasáin 1994, p. 19).

During the last few decades of conflict in the North, decolonizing discourse has come to be associated with the republican political party Sinn Féin, although they by no means have a monopoly on the ideology associated with this discourse. Irish gained a very high profile in the North during the republican prisoners' hunger strike in 1981, partly because the first man to die, Bobby Sands, was an Irish speaker, and partly due to the increasingly widespread use of the Irish language to communicate amongst republican prisoners in Long Kesh. Sinn Féin's involvement with the language throughout the 1980s contributed a great deal to the current shape of decolonizing discourse, which is perhaps best typified by much of the rhetoric of Sinn Féin and a number of its prominent members.

Decolonizing discourse is aggressively nationalist and highly politicized, focusing on the language as a tool to achieve independence from Britain and reunification with the rest of Ireland. National language discourse focuses on developing a sense of national or ethnic identity, but not necessarily in contrast to Ireland's powerful neighbour. Language attitude surveys in the South have shown a strong set of opinions in relation to 'beliefs and feelings about Irish as a focus of ethnic or national identity' (Ó Riagáin and Ó Gliasáin 1994, pp. 18–19). In earlier years, national language discourse bore a stronger resemblance to decolonizing discourse. More recently, especially since the 1980s, the two have diverged more noticeably.

Certain key words, concepts and arguments indicate the use of decolonizing discourse: 'resistance' or 'cultural resistance', 'oppression', 'reconquest', Irish as a 'weapon', and cultural 'struggle', particularly as part of a wider anti-colonial struggle. Often a strong association is made with republican ideals or beliefs. Discourses of anti-imperialism, de-colonization, or political struggle are frequently used in association with the Irish language. Connections are often explicitly made between a person's nationalist political development and his or her interest in the language. Speaking and learning Irish are seen as political acts. Speaking Irish is also seen as a particularly powerful expression of national, and not simply ethnic, identity.

By way of comparison, key words and concepts that indicate the use of national language discourse include 'identity', 'national' or 'ethnic identity', and 'crisis of identity'. There is sometimes an emphasis on pride in one's own culture as a prerequisite for being able to respect the cultures of others. Users of this discourse frequently talk about making Irish people the centre of their own world, and the ability of the Irish language to help achieve this. The idea that a knowledge of both Irish and English would contribute to creative solutions to Ireland's social problems is also a common theme. Finally, users of this discourse sometimes assert that Irish people have a deep-seated sense of inferiority and insecurity about their identity, and that this is related in some way to the plight of the language.

Cultural discourse north and south have the same historical roots, and sit on the opposite side of the ideological fence from decolonizing discourse in particular. Cultural discourse today tends to come in two guises. In the first it tends to be less political, drawing heavily from Romantic and sometimes cultural nationalist ideals. An example of this version is the way a Belfast teacher explains his interest in learning Irish: 'I'd always promised myself to learn Irish and speak it, not through any sort of identity crisis, but because in it I find a certain inherent beauty and a different perspective for looking at the world'. In its second guise, cultural discourse has a definite political agenda, most often in favour of a community relations approach to solving the conflict in the North and strongly against republicanism.

The clearest and most dominant feature of cultural discourse (north) is the assertion that the Irish language and politics should be kept separate. The corollary is that the importance of the language lies in its beauty and cultural worth, not its political capital. The term 'politics' can have a number of different meanings, depending on the context and the speaker. Often it is used as a euphemism for republican politics, with little condemnation made if Irish is associated with other political viewpoints. A more general meaning is party or sectarian politics, the idea being that the language should not be used to further the agenda of any one political party, nor should it be used as a tool in the often sectarian nature of politics in the North.

The central focus of both forms of cultural discourse is on the cultural value of Irish as a unique language, part of the heritage of the Irish people. This does not necessarily indicate a practical desire to learn the language to fluency, nor to see a widespread revival of its use in daily life. As with cultural discourse (north), in the South this discourse is also commonly used to explain an interest in the language, or an interest in having one's children learn the language. While in the North cultural discourse is often used to justify an apolitical position regarding the language, this is a less prominent feature of cultural discourse in the South.

As with decolonizing discourse, there are certain key words, concepts and arguments that indicate the use of cultural discourse (north): 'apolitical', 'depoliticize', 'inclusive', 'tolerance', 'understanding', 'access', 'multiculturalism', 'pluralism', 'beautiful language', 'heritage' or 'common heritage' and 'cultural traditions' (as distinct from traditions in general). Cultural discourse (north) is often used in conjunction with the discourse of community relations. Accusations that the language is being politicized, or attacks on specific individuals or groups for politicizing Irish, figure prominently. A connection is frequently made between a person's interest in Irish and its history, songs and literature. Speaking Irish is generally seen as a cultural activity, and it tends to be seen as an expression of ethnic or cultural identity in contrast to the more dangerous and divisive political or nationalist expressions of identity.

Cultural discourse (south) also includes similar phrases such as 'beautiful language', 'heritage' or 'Gaelic/Celtic heritage', and 'tradition'. A connection is sometimes made between a person's interest in the language, and history, songs and literature in Irish. There is often a distancing from nationalism or any possible political implications of an interest in the language. Speaking Irish is generally seen as a cultural activity, and may be considered a hobby or pastime.

Rights discourse in the North and minority language discourse in the South are comparatively recent, and have therefore developed in quite different socio-political contexts. Still, there are strong parallels between the two. If decolonizing and cultural discourses in Northern Ireland can be seen as constituting two sides of a debate about the relationship between politics and the Irish language, then rights discourse can be seen as a means to side-step this debate and to open up new ideological avenues. In rights discourse, there are two key, inter-connected elements which make it less straightforward than the other two discourses. The first element centres around efforts to break out of the confines of the political/apolitical dichotomy established by decolonizing and cultural discourses. In these discourses the terms of debate are more or less agreed – should politics be kept separate from the Irish language, or is the language an integral part of political struggle? In rights discourse, issues that lead into political/apolitical deadlock are side-stepped through a variety of different strategies: for example, arguments favouring the 'multipoliticization' of Irish, as well as other techniques of avoidance.

The second element centres around efforts to broaden and reframe the debate over politics and the Irish language. In recent years this has been achieved primarily through the issue of rights for Irish speakers. Discourses of civil rights, human rights and minority rights have been adapted as a means of campaigning for the language and developing an ideology that attempts to break out of the confines of the political/apolitical dichotomy.

It seems that in recent years people have begun to see the existing conventions of the political/apolitical debate as overly restrictive and not representative of the way they were feeling about the Irish language and the political situation in Northern Ireland. It has become clear, for example, that many people see the Irish language as significant to their own political beliefs and to the political situation in Northern Ireland as a whole, without seeing the language in direct association with republicanism. This is problematic if the accepted conventions of discourse fix the language in either an apolitical position, or as an important element of cultural resistance to British rule as defined by republicanism. Challenges to this dichotomy have made it easier to express a view associating Irish with politics in the wider sense, without it automatically being associated with republicanism. Instead of being depoliticized, the ideological associations made with the Irish language are being expanded and 'multipoliticized'.

Talk of civil rights for Irish speakers is commonly associated with rights discourse, especially with reference to the funding of Irish schools and the right to use Irish when in contact with the state (for example, on census forms, in court, and in government offices). Comparisons are often made with the status of Welsh and Scots Gaelic as a way of asserting that the British government is discriminating against Irish speakers and, by implication, all Irish people in Northern Ireland. Connections are also made with the issue of minority rights in a European context. Rights discourse is particularly strong in calls for parity of esteem, and in the process of elevating the Irish language to the position of litmus test for equality for nationalists. It resonates with Irish speakers and many non-Irish speaking nationalists alike, making it a fairly powerful voice in current debates.

In the South, minority language discourse has come into its own since the Republic of Ireland joined the European Union. The idea of a 'Europe of the regions' appeals to many people – and to many *Gaeilgeoirí* in particular – because it offers an opportunity for the Irish language to be seen not as a backward, useless language, but as one of many minority and regional languages which are valued and protected within a united Europe. It offers a context in which small and non-universal is acceptable, even desirable. It also allows the focus to be shifted away from the English-speaking world towards a multilingual world, a world where many people speak two or more languages, often their own minority language along with a more 'universal' language such as French or Spanish.

Minority language discourse can be contrasted with national language discourse. It involves a shift not only in strategies for reviving Irish, but a change in the way the language is imagined in relation to Irish identity. While a national language needs no special protection, a minority language does. The rights of its speakers must be respected and even defended in the face of the onslaught of majority language and culture. Perhaps for this reason, minority language discourse bears some relation to rights discourse in the North. As I discuss elsewhere (O'Reilly 1999), reference to Irish as a minority language in the context of Europe has been used as one strategy to secure funding and equal status for the Irish language in Northern Ireland. It can serve a similar purpose in the South, and minority language discourse sometimes features in campaigns to fund Irish language projects.

An important difference between rights and minority language discourse is the status of the former as an oppositional discourse. Minority language discourse has featured in the literature of Irish government authorities such as *Bord na Gaeilge*, while rights discourse often involves an antagonistic stance towards the British government.

Minority language discourse seeks support and protection for the Irish language in the wider context of European minority languages. Rights discourse seeks support for the language and rights for its speakers in three arenas – the United Kingdom, Ireland and Europe – depending on the context.

The emphasis on rights can be traced to the British context in which the Irish language revival in Northern Ireland operates. The movement in the North has been strongly influenced by the Catholic civil rights movement of the 1960s, as well as campaigns for the rights of Welsh and Scots Gaelic speakers. Rights for Irish speakers has been an issue in the Republic also, particularly in the *Gaeltachtaí* during the late 1960s and early 1970s, but this appears to be due at least in part to influences from the fledgling civil rights movement in the North. Kiberd (1995) suggests that both the civil rights movement in the North of Ireland and the *cearta sibhialta* movement spawned in the Connemara *Gaeltacht* were inspired by the movement for black emancipation in the United States.

Rights discourse is signalled by key words, concepts and arguments: 'rights', 'civil rights' and 'human rights', 'equality', 'parity of esteem', the responsibility of government to support minority cultures and uphold minority rights, and a denial that Irish can be wholly apolitical in the current socio-political context of Northern Ireland. Importantly, the promotion of Irish is put above all other political and cultural considerations. The key phrase which indicates the use of minority language discourse is 'minority language', a descriptive term which is unlikely to appear in either cultural discourse (south) or national language discourse. Europe often provides the context in which the discourse is used, and Irish is frequently juxtaposed implicitly or explicitly with other lesser-used or regional languages in the European Union. Practicalities tend to take precedence over intangibles – the topic of discussion is more likely to be business development than identity.

Strictly speaking, dead language discourse is not a discourse of the revival movement, and I will deal with it only briefly. Based on the premise that the Irish language is beyond redemption, dead language discourse is important because it forms and expresses an ideology that *Gaeilgeoirí*, particularly in the South, must oppose. There is a focus on the lack of utility of the Irish language in this discourse, particularly in light of EU membership. Other European languages are seen as more useful, particularly English which provides certain advantages in many parts of the world. Dead language discourse tends also to be profoundly anti-nationalist, perceiving the language as part of a set of conservative forces in Ireland – extreme Catholicism, right-wing nationalism, and the xenophobic attitudes that have often accompanied the discourses of the Irish-language revival in the past.

Dead language discourse is found both north and south of the border, but it is much more prevalent in the Republic. This is due at least in part to negative experiences with the language that many young people have while in school. In contrast, negative attitudes towards the language among Nationalists in Northern Ireland tend to manifest themselves as indifference rather than hostility.

The highly politicized context of Northern Ireland has had a significant impact on the discourses of the North and their associated ideologies. Yet it is clear that *Gaeilgeoirí* both north and south of the border draw on the same historical and ideological material in the formation of discourses on the Irish language, resulting in some similar features. Making a clear distinction between northern and southern discourses is not always an easy matter. I have already commented on the similarities between cultural discourse north and south, and the common use of Europe as a context and framework. At times, the distinction between decolonizing discourse and national language discourse is blurred as well.

In spite of their common historical roots, the discourses have developed in distinct directions as the social and political contexts in the North and the Republic of Ireland diverged post-partition. The result is that although they have certain common features, the discourses are now characterized by different ideologies and tend to be used in different ways. Changes which have affected both parts of Ireland have had different effects on the discourses of the revival: for example, the increasing economic and political importance of Europe.

In Northern Ireland the discourses have developed in the context of a direct political relationship between Irish people in the North, the Unionist population and Britain. A segment of the nationalist population in the North believe that learning and speaking Irish underlines their distinct identity in open contrast to British cultural and political hegemony.

Although political ties between Britain and the Republic of Ireland have been largely severed, many people in the South still feel the need to heal wounds they perceive as being inflicted by the English in the past, most especially the loss of the Irish language. There may be no direct British political presence to struggle against, but some Irish people believe that England's cultural and economic influence in

Ireland is still strong. The 'inferiority complex' or 'weakness' that so many Irish speakers in the South refer to seems to be the southern counterpart of the northern desire to underline their Irishness in the face of British cultural and political hegemony. In the absence of direct political domination by Britain but in light of continuing economic and cultural influences, and in the context of Ireland's changing position in Europe and the wider world, southerners have become engaged in a collective ethnic reassessment. For some, the relevance of the Irish language is a key part of this reassessment.

Irish identity, the Irish language and the European Union

Ó Riagáin (1991) argues that the European Union[14] has not developed a fully comprehensive policy for dealing with the linguistic dimension of European integration. Through programmes such as LINGUA the EU has sought to promote the teaching and learning of foreign languages in order to improve communication between citizens of EU countries, but this does not include a special focus on minority languages. The European Parliament has adopted a number of resolutions over the years in support of regional and minority languages, and the European Bureau for Lesser Used Languages was established to help promote them. Nevertheless, he concludes that the EU is 'unlikely to become a significant influence on language policies and practices of Ireland' (Ó Riagáin 1991, p. 274).

This conclusion rather depends on what is meant by a 'significant influence'. If by this Ó Riagáin means that EU membership is unlikely to inspire a great deal of official change in terms of radically new government policies and initiatives, then he appears to be right. In the Republic of Ireland, government officials have been all too happy to pass the responsibility for finding ways to protect the Irish language onto agencies of the European Union, rather than attempting to formulate new strategies of its own that might prove controversial or unpopular.[15] In Northern Ireland, as we have seen, EU membership has given some leverage to groups campaigning for UK government support for language initiatives. Although the British government was reluctant to sign the European Charter for Regional or Minority Languages,[16] they finally signed up in March 2000 and have been increasingly willing in recent years to consider support for the Irish language as part of peace initiatives in the North. EU support for the Belfast Irish-medium primary school *Bunscoil an Droichead*, when DENI financial support was not forthcoming, sent a clear message about increasing support for Irish-medium education.

It is clear that EU membership has had a significant, if subtle, impact on the fortunes of the Irish language in both parts of Ireland. This impact is not just in terms of changes in policy, but in orientation towards the state and attitudes on the part of the both the government and the populace. In Ireland as a whole, there has been a turning away from a focus on the idealized nation-state and towards Europe. Increasingly, Irish people take a flexible approach in turning towards both or either in terms of identity, sources of financial support and expressions of belief about the Irish language, as evidenced by the discourses discussed above.

There are, of course, differences in degree and, to a certain extent, kind of impact the EU has had on orientation towards the state north and south of the border. Delanty argues that 'European integration has not to any significant extent displaced the nation-state as the normative reference point for people in Northern Ireland' (1996, p. 127). This is true for the most part. Nevertheless, people are prepared to use EU membership and pronouncements on minority languages in an instrumental way, for example, to support their claims for funding and recognition for Irish-language initiatives.

The EU has had a comparatively greater influence in the Republic of Ireland, although it is not clear just how much greater. In the foreword to 'Why Irish?', Tovey, Hannan and Abramson (1989) take a fairly optimistic view, considering that Irish may well fare better in the 'linguistic and cultural mosaic' of modern Europe. They argue that a turning away from narrow conceptions of nationalism might allow a new conception of Irish identity in which the language has a clear and important role, and that EU membership might be a part of this. Yet, CILAR/ITÉ surveys results show minimal optimism on the part of the Irish public – nearly half the population believe the EU membership 'will contribute greatly to the loss of Irish' (Ó Riagáin 1997, p. 176).

Placing the Irish language in a European context, rather than simply the national context, has become increasingly common among Irish-language activists in the South. For example, *Comhar*, an Irish-medium magazine, often examines the language in a European context. *Bord na Gaeilge* recently promoted participation in a European Commission competition called Euroblas, designed to encourage the use of lesser-used languages in the private sector. Minority language discourse has become quite prominent in *Bord na Gaeilge* literature, often appearing alongside national language discourse:

In calling for a refurbishing of Irish identity we suggest that the Irish
language has an integrating and stimulating role to play. This is by
no means a plea for a return to the outlook of the narrow nativistic
ideology of the revivalists, current in the early twentieth century.
Neither is it to favour Irish as opposed to English; indeed we are for-
tunate in having one of the major languages of the world. Rather it
seeks for a sense of confidence in our uniqueness within a polyethnic Europe. A process of revitalising Irish identity could perhaps
espouse a new and serious political neutrality, reflect a sophisticated
distrust of modern hidden imperialisms, show solidarity with the
Third World, show a strong tendency towards humanism and egali-
tarianism, and, in re-examining Irish history, transcend any myopic
preoccupation with the grievances of the past. In any event the construction of a modern Irish identity should affirm those values and
outlooks which are positive, universal and liberating and be seen as
a positive contribution to the evolution of the community of
nations. (*Bord na Gaeilge* 1986: xxxiv–xxxvi)

This passage begins with a plea for a 'refurbished' Irish identity.
Drawing on national language discourse, the Irish language is seen as
vital to achieving this. Irish is then tied in with Ireland's place as part
of a 'polyethnic Europe'. The wording is self-consciously liberal, juxta-
posing this new Irish identity with neutrality, humanism and an
ability to transcend the past – probably a veiled reference to the revival
movement's former preoccupation with Ireland's colonial past and the
tendency to see the Irish language and Irish identity primarily in
contrast with the English language and English identity. At the end of
the passage, the Irish language is seen as playing a key role in establishing a new Irish identity which will shape Ireland's place in the
'community of nations'.

Imagining Irish within the wider framework of Europe is a common
theme in the discussions I have had with individuals involved with the
language in Dublin. People often talk about Irish as a minority language within Europe, sometimes with a sense of pride at their status as
minority language speakers. Occasionally, people feel the need to
defend the importance of Irish when they talk about Europe. A popular
argument against the teaching of Irish in schools is that other
European languages such as German or French would be much more
useful for a child to learn. It is fairly common to hear Irish speakers
bring this point up, even unsolicited. Generally speaking they
acknowledge the importance of these other languages, but then make a

plea for the necessity of a strong Irish identity lest Ireland be overshadowed by its larger and more powerful European neighbours. In the words of one Dublin resident:

> I don't honestly hold a hope of Ireland returning to a Gaelic speaking nation, but I think in recent years ... there's an upsurge of people wanting to learn it [Irish], especially in working class areas – a kind of 'go back to their roots' type of thing, because they're afraid that their identity is going to be lost in the European Community, that everybody else has their identity, where's the Irish going to be? It's creating an upsurge back towards Irish and the whole cultural aspect.

An *Irish Times* journalist investigating the rise in popularity of Irish-medium education in Dublin received some similar responses. As one person told her:

> It's because of multi-channel television. ... It's because we're in the EC. They see that other people speak their own languages. So why not us? (*Irish Times* 13–09–93)

Clearly, EU membership has had implications for Irish identity and attitudes towards the Irish language. Attitudes are shifting in both parts of Ireland, although in somewhat different directions. In the North the politics of culture that have characterized the political process since the ceasefires of 1994 have in many ways led to an intensification of the association between the Irish language and nationalism, while at the same time many Irish language activists have turned to Europe to support their claims for recognition. In the South, a developing politics of identity has become increasingly sceptical of nationalism and more Europeanist in orientation. In both parts of the island, strategies for obtaining support for the language have changed, with appeals increasingly being based on the idea of minority rights in a European context.

Conclusions

The Irish language has been linked to Irish identity in various ways for centuries. The development of an association between Irish and nationalism during the nineteenth century has had a definitive impact on both the fortunes of the language and on the evolution of Irish identity. Partition brought about a divergence in attitudes towards the language and strategies for its revival and eventually in the ways in which the language is imagined in relation to an Irish identity. Different political and social circumstances are reflected in different preoccupations in the discourses of the revival movement, generating similar yet distinctive conceptions of the language in relation to politics, culture and identity.

Membership of the European Union has had differing implications for Ireland north and south of the border. Its effects appear to be stronger in the Republic of Ireland, where a European identity has been embraced by many – especially *Gaeilgeoirí* – as a new context in which to redefine their national identity. The European context has proved to be much more minority language friendly than the previous contexts of first colonialism and then independence in the shadow of the United Kingdom. Meanwhile, in Northern Ireland, EU membership has been exploited instrumentally to further the aims of the revival movement. Yet the full range of possible implications is only just beginning to be explored in the new and still fragile environment of reconciliation. Perhaps the most ironic consequence is that while EU membership has tended to loosen the connection between nationalism and the Irish language in the South, it has served to strengthen this association in the North, as the Irish language becomes ever more firmly a part of Catholic/nationalist political and cultural identity.

Notes

1. For a concise history of the fortunes of Irish, see Crowley (1996), Chapter 4. For a more detailed history of the politics of Irish from the fourteenth century to the founding of the Irish Free State, see Crowley (2000).
2. Significantly, this third phase coincides with the entry of the Republic of Ireland into the EC in 1972.
3. See Ó Riagáin (1997), Chapter 6, for details.
4. Since the founding of the state, Irish has been a required subject in all government-funded schools, though since 1973 it is no longer a compulsory subject in public examinations.
5. See Lee (1989), Farrell (1980) and Hennessy (1997) for different historical accounts of the position of Catholics in Northern Ireland, while O'Connor (1993) offers an interesting insight into the views of Catholics in the North.
6. For information about Protestants and the Irish language in Northern Ireland, see McCoy (1997) and Ó Snodaigh (1995).
7. During the 1950s and 1960s, 11 couples from Belfast who were involved with the Irish-language movement met and married. They came together to house their young families on what was then the outskirts of west Belfast,

forming the first urban neo-*Gaeltacht* in Ireland and later starting Northern Ireland's first Irish-medium primary school, *Bunscoil Phobal Feirste*. When interest in the language began to increase in the 1980s, the Shaws Road *Gaeltacht* became the foundation of the revival movement. See Maguire (1991) for a detailed discussion of the Shaws Road.

8. To help encourage progress in the peace process and political negotiations, the European Union started a peace and reconciliation fund to promote cultural and educational projects in the North. Some of this money has been funnelled through the Department of Education to support new *bunscoileanna* during the early years of their development. The three schools receiving such funding to date are: *Bunscoil an Droichead* in Belfast, *Bunscoil Dhál Riada* in County Antrim, and *Bunscoil Luraigh* in County Derry.

9. At time of writing, there were two Irish-medium secondary schools in the North, one in Belfast and one in Derry. A second school for Belfast is in the planning stages, and may be open for the 2001–2 school year. There has been talk for a number of years of another secondary school in a more rural location south of Belfast, but this has not yet materialized.

10. As of 1999–2000, there are 1441 pupils in Northern Ireland's *bunscoileanna* (primary schools) and 384 pupils in the *meánscoileanna* (secondary schools). Approximately 600 children attend the *naíonraí* (Irish-medium nursery schools). (Figures supplied by *Gaeloiliúint*.)

11. See O'Reilly (1996) for a discussion of the role of the Irish language in the peace process, and O'Reilly (2000) for an examination of the politics of culture that has come to dominate the political scene in Northern Ireland in recent years.

12. Irish language organizations have increasingly moved from campaign focused groups to institutions of the state since the 1990s. As part of the political process in the North, a number of new bodies have recently been established. These include *An Foras Teanga*, a cross-border body to promote the Irish language that incorporates *Bord na Gaeilge*, which used to have jurisdiction only in the Republic; *Comhairle na Gaelscolaíocht*, an educational board financed by the Department of Education (Northern Ireland) to oversee the Irish-medium schools sector; and *Ciste na Gaelscolaíocht*, a committee responsible for capital fundraising for Irish-medium schools and other Irish language projects.

13. See O'Reilly (1999) for a more in-depth discussion.

14. For clarity I use the term 'European Union' to refer to the current and previous incarnations of this entity, including the European Community as it was known when Ó Riagáin (1991) was writing.

15. For example, the Republic of Ireland has given ongoing financial support to the European Bureau for Lesser Used Languages since the early 1980s, even as its own strategies for promoting the language fell into a period of 'stagnation and retreat' (to quote P. Ó Riagáin). Another consequence of EU membership is that there is now another source of funding for Irish language initiatives aside from the Irish government – the EU budget line B3-1006 (Regional Languages and Cultures).

16. The UK was one of five countries that abstained from supporting the Charter at the original vote of the CAHLR in 1981. 21 countries voted in favour (see D. Ó Riagáin, this volume).

Bibliography

Andrews, L.S. BBC Northern Ireland and the Irish Language: the Background, in *BBC agus an Ghaeilge*/BBC and the Irish language, A. Mac Póilin and L. Andrews, eds (Belfast: *Iontaobhas ULTACH*/ULTACH Trust, 1992).

Andrews, L.S. 'The very dogs in the streets will bark in Irish': The Unionist Government and the Irish language 1921–43, in *The Irish Language in Northern Ireland*, A. Mac Póilin, ed. (Belfast: *Iontaobhas ULTACH*/ULTACH Trust, 1997).

Bord na Gaeilge, The Irish Language in a Changing Society: shaping the future (Dublin: The Advisory Planning Committee, 1989).

Cathcart, R. *The Most Contrary Region: the BBC in Northern Ireland 1924–1984* (Belfast: Blackstaff Press, 1984).

Crowley, T. *Language in History: Theories and Texts* (London: Routledge, 1996).

Crowley, T. *The Politics of Language in Ireland: 1366–1922* London: Routledge, 2000).

Delanty, G. Northern Ireland in a Europe of Regions. *Political Quarterly* 67:2 (1996) 127–34.

Farrell, M. *Northern Ireland: the Orange State* (London: Pluto Press, 1980).

Fichte, J.G. *Addresses to the German Nation* [1808]. G. Armstrong Kelly (ed.) (New York: Harper, 1968).

Hennessy, T. *A History of Northern Ireland 1920–1996* (Basingstoke: Macmillan – now Palgrave, 1997).

Hindley, R. *The Death of the Irish Language: a Qualified Obituary* (London: Routledge, 1990).

Lee, J J. *Ireland 1912–1985: Politics and Society* (Cambridge: Cambridge University Press, 1989).

Mac Póilin, A. *Aspects of the Irish Language Movement in Northern Ireland*. Unpublished paper presented at Language Policy and Planning in the European Union Conference, Institute of Irish Studies, University of Liverpool, 29 April (1995).

Maguire, G. *Our Own Language: an Irish Initiative. Multilingual Matters* 66 (1991). Clevedon: Multilingual Matters, Ltd.

McCoy, G. Protestant Learners of Irish in Northern Ireland, in *The Irish language in Northern Ireland*, A. Mac Póilin (ed.). (Belfast: *Iontaobhas ULTACH*/ULTACH Trust, 1997).

O'Connor, F. *In Search of a State: Catholics in Northern Ireland* (Belfast: The Blackstaff Press, 1993).

Ó Donnaile, A. Can Linguistic Minorities Cope with a Favourable Majority?, in *The Irish language in Northern Ireland*, A. Mac Póilin (ed.). (Belfast: *Iontaobhas ULTACH*/ULTACH Trust, 1997).

O'Reilly, C. The Irish Language – Litmus Test for Equality? Competing Discourses of Identity, Parity of Esteem, and the Peace Process. *Irish Journal of Sociology* 6(1996), 154–78.

O'Reilly, C. *The Irish Language in Northern Ireland: the Politics of Culture and Identity* (Basingstoke: Macmillan – now Palgrave, 1999).

O'Reilly, C. The Politics of Culture in Northern Ireland, In J. Neuheiser (ed.) *Breakthrough to Peace? The Impact of the Good Friday Agreement on Northern Irish Politics and Society* (New York and Oxford: Berghahn, 2002).

Ó Riagáin, P. and Ó Gliasáin, M. *National Survey on Languages 1993: Preliminary Report.* Research Report 18 (Dublin: Institiúid Teangeolaíochta Eireann, 1994).

Ó Riagáin, P. National and International Dimensions of Language Policy When the Minority Language is a National Language: the Case of Irish in Ireland, in F. Coulmas (ed.) *A Language Policy for the European Community: Prospects and Quandaries* (New York: Mouton de Gruyter, 1991).

Ó Riagáin, P. *Language Policy and Social Reproduction: Ireland 1893–1993* (Oxford: Oxford University Press, 1997).

Ó Snodaigh, T. *Hidden Ulster: Protestants and the Irish Language* (Belfast: Lagan Press, 1995).

Tovey, H., Hannan, D. and Abramson, H. *Why Irish? Irish Identity and the Irish Language* (Dublin: *Bord na Gaeilge*, 1989).

6
Ethnic Identity and Minority Language Survival in Brittany

Lenora Timm

Introduction

Comment peut-on être breton? [How can one be Breton?] Such was the trenchant title of an influential book by Breton journalist Morvan Lebesque (1970) in which the author explores how, or whether, Bretons, and other ethnic minorities in France, can maintain a sense of cultural identity within that highly centralized state. Lebesque's perspective is that Bretons, and other minorities in France, are colonized peoples, reflecting the socio-political theorizing of the day regarding 'internal colonization' (see Hechter 1975; Reece 1977); he argues against any essentialist component of Breton identity, concluding that a sense of 'Bretonness' is, in the end, *'une conscience et une volonté d'être'* ['a consciousness and a will to be'] (1970, p. 219). This chapter looks again at Lebesque's question, for it continues to be of interest 30 years later. The world has changed in many ways since 1970, and the definition, or in today's terms, construction, of cultural identities has taken on new dimensions. Understanding Breton identity in France and Europe at the turn of the twenty-first century is, in other words, a project that merits revisiting, for identities are always changing as humans adjust to new conditions and realities in their social and physical environments. However, as will be shown, Lebesque's assessment about the general nature of Breton identity finds resonance in some of the perspectives offered by Bretons today that are set forth later in this chapter.

Exploring common designators of identity

Any discussion of cultural/political identity leads immediately to an encounter in the literature with a variety of designators, sometimes deployed with little or no definition. For the purposes of this chapter, I will limit myself to examining four terms that seem of particular relevance in discussing the Breton case: *nation, state, ethnicity,* and *identity.*

Nation

The term *nation* and congeners (*national, nationality, nationalism*) all refer in their etymological origins to place of birth; those of a given *natio* were, to the Romans, born in the same locale – a city or piece of land; a unit larger than a family but smaller than a clan or people (Zernatto 1944, p. 352). In today's understanding, a nation generally means a community of people sharing in certain cultural and historical traditions, socio-political and administrative structures and enjoying some measure of autonomy. Additionally, a shared language has often been considered a crucial component of nationhood; this was particularly true in eighteenth to nineteenth century formulations of the concept.

I find the more encompassing definition provided by social anthropologist Lois Kuter (1985) to be useful here:

> A 'nation' is a population which shares a common culture, or thinks it does, and desires self-determination or ultimate decision-making power for itself. (p. 20)

This definition does not emphasize language, and under-specifies 'self-determination or ultimate decision-making power', which may range from full sovereignty, or the desire for it, to regional authority over various economic, social and educational matters. In any event, by this definition, Brittany is a nation, since its people share in a common culture and history; and, at least in the eyes of activists in the Breton movement (see page 119, below), it is interested in self-determination. Some activists are, or have been, separatists; while other activists, the majority, desire more regional autonomy for Brittany. However, among many Breton people, the term, especially as embedded in 'nationalist' and 'nationalism', is avoided, having been 'tainted' by the ideology and activities of a small coterie of collaborationist-separatists during the second world war. Elsewhere in Europe, 'national' is commonly used in referring to well-established minority groups.

In contrast with 'nation', 'state' designates a hegemonic political structure with legal authority over a territory that may encompass a spectrum of socio-cultural groups, quite possibly including 'nations'. Barbour (1996, p. 28) comments that 'At the level of polities [,] states generally describe themselves as nations, and their status as nations is crucial to their legitimacy', whence the designator 'nation-state' – of which France is an example *par excellence.*

Ethnic/ethnicity

According to Chapman, McDonald and Tonkin (1989, pp. 14–15), the term 'ethnic' came into widespread employment in its modern sense following WW II, replacing certain others that had become more offensive, such as 'racial' or 'tribal'; these scholars describe it as a term very much like 'race' but without the biology, though the latter may still creep in. There is no dearth of definitions for 'ethnic group' or 'ethnicity'. One, the focus of an earlier study of the Breton movement (Timm 1988), was drawn from Smith (1981):

> a social group whose members share a sense of common origins, claim a common and distinctive history and destiny, possess one or more distinctive characteristics, and feel a sense of collective uniqueness and solidarity. (p. 66)

Added to this was the fact that ethnic groups are generally thought to consist of people 'linked to one another by "primordial" ties of kinship, religion, custom, and until the twentieth century, of language', with the qualifier that 'not all contemporary Bretons are especially interested in their ethnicity and may even repudiate it, or, perhaps, claim co-allegiance to France and accept that their destiny is bound up with the latter's' (1988, p. 21).

Today, I find myself less inclined than before to depict Bretons as an ethnicity. For one reason, the term itself, along with 'ethnic group' has undergone a measure of semantic pejoration. As Chapman, McDonald, and Tonkin remark:

> It is a term that half-heartedly aspires to describe phenomena that involve everybody, and that nevertheless has settled in the vocabulary as a marker of strangeness and unfamiliarity. (1989, p. 16)

That is, it is altogether too easy for a dominant majority to see itself as having *no* ethnicity, a quality which is attributed by the latter only to minority groups. Moreover, the definition I relied on earlier does not seem fully applicable to Bretons today, a perspective shared by some other researchers on Breton terrain. For example, Le Coadic (1998,

p. 46) argues that Bretons do not constitute an ethnic group because Brittany has traditionally been inhabited by *two* distinct groups speaking different languages – a Breton-speaking people in Lower Brittany and a French- or Gallo-speaking people in Upper Brittany (see page 109, below, for the distinction). Another Breton scholar, Rannou (1987), considers that the majority of Bretons have so assimilated to French culture that it is no longer possible to speak of the Bretons as a group with a distinctive identity, with the possible exception of the *militants marginalisés* [marginalized militants] (ibid., p. 18). Finally, as will be discussed later, such notions as 'primordial ties' of kinship do not necessarily resonate with Bretons in today's world.

Identity

The term identity has two senses: an essentialist one whereby an individual or group possesses something in and of itself; and a sense in which identity, like ethnicity, draws its meaning from oppositions and relativities (Chapman, McDonald and Tonkin 1989, p. 17). For most researchers today who are concerned with classifying people, 'a group or individual has no *one* identity, but a variety (a potentially very large variety), of possibilities, that only incompletely or partially overlap in social time and space' (ibid.). Moreover, identity is dynamic, flexible and subject to change.

> In light of these observations, the following description of Breton identity seems apt: Breton identity is best described not as an 'ethnic' identity, but as a geographic/cultural/social/political identity varying from one individual to another according to that individual's personal experiences, interactions with others, and values. (Kuter 1985, p. 23)

Further characterizations of Breton identity will be examined on pages 113--19.

Brittany: a small nation within the nation-state *par excellence*

There has long been a mystique associated with Brittany, this westernmost portion of the French 'Hexagon'.[1] In centuries past, visitors from other countries and from more urbanized areas of France were both fascinated and repelled by this area, describing it in largely negative terms as isolated, backward, with 'savage' landscapes and equally 'savage' inhabitants speaking a bizarre and arcane tongue. This passage from Victor Hugo's novel *Quatre-vingt treize* [1793] describing the Breton peasant gives the flavour:

> *sauvage grave et singulier, cet homme á l'oeil clair et aux cheveux longs, vivant de lait et de châtaignes, borné a son toit de chaume ... ne servant de l'eau que pour boire ... parlant une langue morte ... aimant ses rois, ses seigneurs, ses prêtres, ses poux.* (quoted in Laîné, 1992, p. 65)

[wild, grave and peculiar, this clear-eyed man with long hair, living off of milk and chestnuts, restricted to his thatched roof ... using water only for drinking ... speaking a dead language, loving his kings, his lords, his priests, his lice]

It was not until the eighteenth century that philological research demonstrated that the indigenous language of the peninsula, Breton, was Celtic, with close genetic links to Cornish and Welsh (the Brythonic group within the Celtic family) and more distant ones to the Gaelic languages of the British Isles (Scots and Irish Gaelic and Manx).

The prevailing interpretation of the origins of this Celtic people on what eventually become French territory is that, from the third to fifth centuries AD, Britons from southern parts of present-day England crossed the English Channel and settled on what was for long called the Armorican Peninsula. It is generally believed that the emigration was motivated by incursions into their original territory by Irish from the west and, later, by Anglo-Saxons from the northeast.[2] This Brythonic-speaking population established a realm that extended as far east as Rennes and as far south as Nantes. Their language evolved into what is now called Breton (*brezhoneg*), the earliest traces of which (seventh to eleventh centuries) are found in proper names and in glosses on Latin manuscripts and cartularies (Gourvil 1968, p. 74).

Space here does not permit more than a cursory summary of the subsequent history of Brittany. Suffice it to say that the peninsula perdured as a network of settlements and eventually as a kingdom independent of the expansionist Frankish rulers and Norse invaders until the early tenth century. It was militarily defeated by French forces in 1488, but retained independence as a duchy until 1532, when Brittany was officially annexed as a province of France (Abalain 1995, pp. 16–17).

The territory of Brittany today consists officially of four departments (Côtes d'Amor, Finistère, Ile-et-Vilaine and Morbihan) but unofficially, and traditionally, there is a fifth Breton department, Loîre-Atlantique, with its important capital city, Nantes.[3] Brittany is also bifurcated geolinguistically, in most descriptions, into Upper Brittany and Lower Brittany: the former comprises the eastern half of the peninsula, where French and a related Romance language, Gallo, have long been spoken; and the latter comprises the western portion of the peninsula, where Breton once predominated.[4] The population of Brittany (including Loîre-Atlantique) is today about 4 million (Broudic 1999; Denez 1998).

Throughout the many centuries of their habitation of the peninsula that precede the present one, the vast majority of Bretons – peasants, artisans, fisherfolk and sailors – were monolingual Breton speakers. The Breton nobility, together with the merchants and professional classes, became bilingual fairly early on, as the need to communicate in French became a necessity for political, administrative and commercial purposes. The nobility gradually abandoned Breton altogether, for many had been marrying into high-ranking Frankish and Norman families.[5] Breton had thus become, by the Middle Ages, a language associated with a largely rural, largely uneducated, population, an association that would continue to the present time (see below).

Although in the sixteenth century, Brittany was annexed to France, the administrators of the French Crown showed relatively little interest in the linguistic habits of the Breton masses (or of those inhabitants of other largely rural areas for that matter). The language flourished as a vernacular (or assemblage of vernaculars, since there was considerable dialect variation across space), while remaining underdeveloped as a literary language until the twentieth century. It was not until the aftermath of the French Revolution of 1789 that the now strongly centrist government began its campaign against Breton and other non-French languages, as well as non-standard varieties of French. For the next nearly 200 years efforts to eliminate these languages and French-related 'patois' would be nearly unremitting. Statements from Republican officials are abundant on the subject of the desirability of what in today's terms might be called the 'linguistic cleansing' of the nation-state. Perhaps the most repeated of these is the one by a Revolutionary official, Barère, in 1794, speaking for the *Comité de Salut Public* (Committee for Public Safety):

Le fédéralisme et la superstition parlent bas-breton; l'emigration et la haine de la République parlent allemand; la contre-révolution parle italien et le fanatisme parle basque. (quoted in Laîné 1992, p. 67)

[Federalism and superstition speak Breton; emigration and hatred of the Republic speak German; the counter-revolution speaks Italian and fanatacism speaks Basque]

Of course he wanted to extirpate these linguistic perils that threatened the safety of the new nation-state. Barrère is also said to have proposed physically eliminating Alsatians from France in order to give an example to all those in France who spoke a 'patois' (ibid., p. 72). Well over a century later, in 1925, the French Minister of Education would declare, 'For the unity of France, the Breton language must disappear' (Timm 1973, p. 297, n. 19).

What was not accomplished by policy and enforcement, much of it via the educational system (see below), was largely accomplished through the technological, economic, political and cultural changes that ensued. Historian Eugen Weber writes:

Roads, railroads, schools, markets, military service, and the circulation of money, goods, and printed matter ... swept away old commitments, instilled a national view of things in regional minds, and confirmed the power of that view by offering advancement to those who adopted it. The national ideology was still diffuse and amorphous around the middle of the nineteenth century. French culture became truly national only in the last years of the century. (1976, p. 486)

French was the carrier of this culture, and smaller languages within the Hexagon were no match for this powerful competitor, which, in any event, was more often than not welcomed by the local populations. It was the vehicle for new ideas, for participation in a dominant ideology, and key to the advancement of one's children. As Favereau (1993, p. 130) observes:

Il est peu contestable que l'adhésion des bretonnants à l'idéologie française ait été réelle, voir enthousiaste, comme ce fut le cas dans de nombreuses autres régions, ou pays colonisés au demeurant, surtout en ce qui concerne l'assimilation par l'éducation, an deskadurezh, mot magique ...

[It is hardly contestable that Breton speakers' adherence to French ideology had been real, even enthusiastic, as was the case in numerous other regions, or colonized countries in general, above all in matters concerning assimilation through education, *an deskadurezh*, a magical word ...]

The results of cultural assimilation and socio-political integration on the language profile of Brittany have been drastic. From an estimated 1.3 million speakers of Breton (many monolingual) at the end of the nineteenth century, the number of Breton speakers has declined to perhaps 240 000 today, with virtually all of these being bilingual, and with only about 10 per cent of them (24 000 people) speaking the language regularly, that is, on a daily basis (Broudic 1999).[6] While an appreciable literary repertoire in Breton has been created in this century, there is only a tiny proportion of the Breton-speaking population who is able to, or who chooses to, read Breton-language publications.

Language and identity in Brittany: historical perspectives

A recurring theme in Weber's (1976) detailed examination of the transformation of consciousness among France's rural populations in the nineteenth century is that it took some time for the country's many 'regions' to develop a sense of belonging to the larger nation-state. Comments from observers (voyagers or military men) of the day make this point very well. For example, in 1880, an English traveller through the Landes, a department in the south-west of France, wrote of the people there that they

> live on French soil but cannot be called Frenchmen. They speak a language as unintelligible to a Frenchman as an Englishman; they have none of the national characteristics – little, perhaps of the national blood. (Weber 1976, p. 97)

Brittany was one of the last regions to be woven into the national tapestry,[7] not only because of its remoteness from the centre, but also because, as noted above, it had enjoyed status as an independent kingdom and then as an autonomous duchy during the early modern period of European history.[8] The nobility, the bourgeoisie, and the Church all possessed a strong sense of Breton distinctiveness in history, culture and language. Catholic clergy, in particular, had long supported the Breton language, understanding its key role in propagating religious and moral values. In fact, the first reference works for Breton were written by or for men of the cloth.[9] Among the people, however, a sense of Breton identity began to emerge largely in reaction to negative stereotyping by outsiders, such as that exemplified in the Victor Hugo passage cited earlier. The government's nineteenth century campaign against Breton in the schools, which was often carried out brutally in both physical and psychological terms,[10] effectively stigmatized the language among its own native speakers, who had precious few resources – academic or political – to combat this sort of linguistic warfare. Pre-WWI generations of Bretons yielded to the negative stereotypes others had created about them. Concerning their traditional language, they accepted that it was, as they had been told, useless outside of their narrow village lives and an impediment to social advancement. As Breton historian Yves Le Gallo puts it:

On comprend que le peuple breton n'ait pas su défendre sa langue. C'était la livrée que lui avaient imposée de siècles d'humilité et d'humiliation, de solitude et d'indigence. (quoted in Le Coadic 1998, p. 206)

[It is understood that the Breton people did not know how to defend its language. This was the burden that centuries of humility and humiliation, of solitude and poverty had imposed on them]

Nevertheless, Breton remained the daily spoken vernacular of the people of Lower Brittany, but, increasingly, along with French. Thus, whereas in 1902 about 50 per cent of that population was monolingual in Breton, by 1950, only 7 per cent were. Also by 1950, three-quarters of Bretons (of Lower Brittany) were bilinguals, with the remaining quarter by then French monolinguals; only a relative handful of ageing Breton monolinguals were still alive (Broudic 1999, p. 19).

During the '30 glorious years' following WWII, the Breton economy (as elsewhere in France) modernized dramatically. There were improvements in transportation and communication systems, the industrialization of agriculture, the installation of light industry, a boom in new housing construction, and the advent of serious tourism. Brittany especially flourished during these years, and developed a reputation for high quality products, many of them agricultural. The regional association called 'Produit en Bretagne' [Made in Brittany] campaigned vigorously and successfully for the marketing of Breton products and services (for example, 'Brittany Ferries') throughout Europe (Le Coadic 1998, p. x).

All these changes went hand in hand with the spread and, more importantly, the intensification of the use of French. To many Bretons, no doubt, the Breton language seemed both irrelevant and disadvantageous. Thus an entire generation of young, bilingual adults who became parents following WWII decided that they would not speak Breton to their babies,[11] though they often continued to speak it with their own parents and perhaps to one another. As a result, most 'baby boomers' in Lower Brittany developed chiefly a receptive competence in Breton: they can understand it but not speak it. The linguistic situation, one of accelerating language shift, has evolved to the point that today 80 per cent of the population of Lower Brittany is monolingual in French; and there are virtually no Breton monolinguals remaining.

In spite of widespread language shift, it seems that many Bretons have maintained a sense of themselves as a distinct people within the boundaries of the French nation-state. What are the parameters of this identity?

Contrasting interpretations of Breton and Celtic identity

It was argued above that cultural/political/individual identities are complex constructions and subject to change over time. In this section I will explore the notion that not only has Breton (and Celtic) identity been constructed of partial and overlapping elements, but that these elements have rather literally been 'invented,' This conceptualization is found in the work of such historians as Anderson (1983) and Hobsbawm (1983); indeed, Hobsbawm argues that national traditions since the French Revolution are in large measure 'exercises in social engineering which are often deliberate and always innovative' (p. 83), and that they merit the serious attention of historians and other researchers. For analysis of the construction of Celtic traditions and nationalisms we may look to such scholars as Chapman (1992), Dietler (1994), Maynard (1997) and McDonald (1989). I will limit further dis- cussion here to the work of McDonald (1989), who has specifically addressed the invention/construction of Breton identity. Space does not permit more than a brief consideration of her arguments, but it is important to address them, for they will strike some as provocative. McDonald's observations will then be contrasted with the ethno- graphic findings of a Breton sociologist (Le Coadic 1998), who has done extensive fieldwork among Bretons of both Lower and Upper

Brittany, in which he explores their views on what it means to be
Breton in today's Brittany.

  McDonald undertook fieldwork in Brittany in the late 1970s to early
1980s, during the course of which she moved, in part, among language
and culture activists – the Breton 'militants'. She is well versed in the
literature by and about Bretons, and Celts in general. To be brief, she
argues (as does Chapman 1992) that Celtic identity has been constructed bit by bit through the centuries. She asks,

> But who, first of all, are the 'Celts' and how were they invented?
> The category 'Celt' travelled a long and rather complicated road
> before finally leaping forth as this ethnic self-ascription on the
> north-western edge of Europe. (1989, p. 99)

She continues,

> They began their recorded life as part of the ethnological bric-à-brac
> of the classical world … eventually filling the entire space of every-
> thing odd, barbaric, or different, they eventually became most
> clearly pinned down, geographically at least in Gaul. (ibid.)

That which is specifically Breton identity, in her view, was forged in
the nineteenth century by 'mostly noblemen, priests, and scholars
strongly opposed to a Republic increasingly anti-clerical in its commitment to the ideals of the 1789 Revolution' (ibid., p. 103). She places
particular emphasis on the publication in 1837 of the collection of oral
literature known as the *Barzaz Breiz* ('Poetry of Brittany') by Theodore
Hersart de la Villemarqué, which offered an image of Brittany as a mys-
terious ancient Celtic land of customs, poetry, and song, far more ven-
erable in its traditions than France. In McDonald's view, Breton
militants of the twentieth century have inherited, savoured and further
elaborated this imagery in opposing all things Celtic to those French –
the Breton language being a prime marker of the former. She insists on
the artificial nature of Breton identity:

> An autonomous minority history [of the Bretons] has been con-
> structed and identity pursued into a distant past according to the
> preoccupations and images of the present. … Post-war sociology
> and events such as 'May '68' in France have given the modern
> Celts a secure place in the relations of majority/minority, centre/
> periphery, colonizer/colonized, exploiter/exploited, and so on. The

symbolically marginal, spiritual Celtic world can now also claim modern political subjection through 'ethnic' studies. (ibid., p. 116)

Following this interpretation, we arrive at a situation in which a militant minority within the overall Breton minority has drawn on elements of an idealized and romanticized history to validate their movement for cultural/linguistic recognition, and which may go as far as a call for political autonomy; while at the same time a non-militant, mainly assimilated, and largely politically apathetic majority of the minority are not much interested in their identity as Bretons.

I do not argue with the notion that history is subject to interpretation as well as manipulation for diverse ends by individuals or groups with conflicting claims or ambitions;[12] or that nations or aspiring groups create symbols (flags, national anthems) and emphasize or simply invent stories that glorify the past and legitimate the *status quo*. However, I am concerned that in laying bare the constructed/invented nature of various national(istic) ideologies and narratives we assume that all sense of identity of a particular people is therefore invented. In short, the deconstructive discourse itself is highly abstract and tells us little about how people – ordinary people – go about representing themselves and perceiving others and the world around them.

While it is important to acknowledge that in their self-representation and their perceptions people are likely to be influenced by elements of invented traditions and ideology, it is nonetheless valid to contemplate whether other factors may be involved and to ask, in the case of Brittany: how do ordinary Bretons today, within their traditional territory, envisage their own identity, and what does it mean to them (if anything)?

This was the overarching question guiding the dissertation research published recently by Ronan Le Coadic (1998), a sociologist at the University of Rennes-2, whose book, *L'identité bretonne* [Breton identity], offers detailed findings of in-depth interviews with 46 'ordinary' Bretons from both Lower and Upper Brittany on this topic. It provides, in my opinion, a down to-earth alternative view, or set of views – from people living their lives in Brittany today – as to what Breton identity means.[13]

Given the relatively small number of respondents, the study does not lend itself to statistically meaningful generalizations, but as a piece of qualitative research, it is an impressive achievement. Le Coadic carried out semi-guided interviews with adult Bretons (from 20–65 years old, the average age being 45). The sample consisted of 17 women and 29 men, working in rural areas, whose occupations were principally in agriculture or fishing. However, a few heads of businesses were also included. The selection of occupation types was deliberate, since Le Coadic believed that people in rural sectors would be more likely to know or be in contact with Breton language and culture (in Lower Brittany) or Gallo language and culture (in Upper Brittany); while the heads of business might provide some interesting contrasting perspectives (1998, pp. 26–7). The interviewees' knowledge of Breton ranged from none (32/46), to comprehension ability (9/46) to full fluency (5/46).

Interview questions were posed orally by the author and included such open-ended queries as the following: '*Que représente dans votre vie personnelle, le fait d'être breton(ne)?*' [What does the fact of being Breton represent in your personal life?] (p. 62). '*Est-ce qu'il vous arrive parfois d'écouter des émissions en breton, soit à la télé, soit à la radio?*' [Do you sometimes listen to broadcasts in Breton, either on TV or on the radio?] (p. 245). '*Aimeriez-vous connaître le breton?*' [Would you like to know Breton?] (p. 214). (These are just a few examples of Le Coadic's questions.) Interviews were audiotaped and subsequently transcribed for analysis. I cannot do justice to the full range of material available in this study of nearly 500 pages, but what follows captures what I regard as some important findings of Le Coadic's study.

From the responses to the question regarding what being Breton means in one's personal life, Le Coadic ascertained that a solid majority of his interviewees (25/46) felt that it was indeed meaningful to them: for example, '*C'est la fierté des racines!*' [It's pride in one's roots!] '*Ma nature de vivre, Ma raison de vivre*' [My way of living, my reason to live] (1998, p. 62). A strong minority (20/46), however, were less decisive: '*Breton, oui, mais non, sans plus*' [Breton, yes, but no, nothing more] (ibid.). Or simply, '*C'est important*' [It's important] (ibid.); no respondents stated that being Breton was a negative attribute.

The Breton language has served as a traditional cultural marker of that identity throughout Brittany. As noted, few in Le Coadic's sample speak the language fluently, though such fluency is often cited by interviewees as an external marker of Bretonness. His respondents were divided on the question of whether or not language is in fact a crucial factor in identity, with more respondents from Upper Brittany (non-Breton speakers) stressing the importance of the Breton language for Breton identity than respondents from Lower Brittany (1998, p. 215).

Le Coadic argues that many interviewees resorted to 'symbolic inversion' to assert the characteristics that they feel make them Breton. Thus, some long-standing stereotypes of Bretons seem to have been assimilated as markers of Bretonness today: 'stubborn', 'primitive', 'rough', 'emotional', 'close to nature', 'heavy drinkers', 'family-oriented'.

If 'primordial ties of kinship' are an element of ethnicity, then these Bretons do not constitute an ethnic group, for many in Le Coadic's sample did not feel that it was necessary to be born in Brittany or be genetically Breton to identify as one. For them, Breton identity can be adopted by individuals who love the territory and the way of life. Identity is thus explicitly disassociated from genetic or deep historical ties, at least for some Bretons.

By contrast, throughout this work there are statements by respondents who place their sense of Bretonness within the context of the *pays* ('locality'), of region, or of soil:

> '*Il y a quand même ce sentiment d'appartenir à quelque chose ... le Breton est rattaché à sa région*' [Anyway, there is a feeling of belonging to something ... the Breton is attached to his/her region'] (p. 321). '*Chacun est différent, mais on est sur un sol qui s'appelle la Bretagne et chacun est conscient de ça*' [Everyone is different, but you are on soil that is called Brittany and everyone is conscious of that]. (p. 322)

This perspective is shared by several scholars who have concerned themselves with Breton identity. For example, for Le Gars, this identity '... *puise ses fondements dans un territoire – écosysteme historique et culturel*' [... has its foundation in a territory – an historical and cultural ecosystem] (1998, p. 21). Favereau (1993) argues that for the Breton, identity is first of all an attachment to *paysage*, to a place. And an attachment of what is picturesque, more than to what is rural (p. 47). One speaks of *patrimoine paysager* [the heritage of landscape] (p. 49). One of the public figures in Le Coadic's study states:

> *On est de ce pays, de ce territoire. ... Et la realité des paysages, des sites et des caractères du paysage bas-breton, je crois que c'est la base de l'identité.* (Le Coadic 1998, p. 65). [One is from this countryside, from this territory. ... And the reality of the landscapes, of the sites and the

character of the Breton landscape, I think that that is the basis of identity].

The theme of the beauty of the Breton landscape is a recurring one among Le Coadic's interviewees, for example (1998, p. 68):

> *C'est magnifique, ces côtes! ... C'est tres beau! Même l'intérieur Bretagne! Il y a tout ici!* [They are magnificent, the coastlines! ... It's very beautiful! Even the interior of Brittany. Everything is here!].

> *Oh, je me dis, quelle belles couleurs! Et quand on voit, sur le bord des routes, les genêts en fleurs, moi je trouve ça formidable.* [Oh, I say to myself, such beautiful colours! And when you see, along the sides of the highways, the broom in flower, I find that fantastic].

> *Où on peut aller pour trouver aussi beau que chez nous? Parce qu'elle est belle notre Bretagne! Avec ses côtes toutes decoupées, les maisons ... c'est nous, quoi!* [Where can you go to find anything so beautiful as we have here? Because our Brittany is beautiful! With its rugged coastlines, the houses ... it's us, you know!].

To the question, what is the basis of Breton identity today?, there is no simple or straightforward answer. Identity is conceptualized by social scientists, and is, I believe, also felt by many who think about it, as a layering or interweaving of components, not reducible to any single dimension of an individual's socio-cultural circumstances or personality. For some Bretons, identity may incorporate elements of earlier stereotyped and/or mythologized versions of Breton and Celtic history (McDonald's [1989] view): to be 'stubborn', 'a dreamer', 'emotional', 'primitive', 'poetic', 'nature-lover', and so on. For others it may mean that one was born in Brittany, displays a Breton flag or BZH ('Brittany') bumper sticker, speaks or desires to speak Breton, or simply that one came to love Breton landscapes, music, *festoù-noz* ('night festivals') and other festivities or the 'way of life'. Individual Bretons will, in short, vary considerably in the bundles of features of identity that they choose to articulate, or display in some way.

Some Bretons will manifest none of these features, and may deny or reject an explicit Breton identity, while perhaps opting for an entirely different one – for example, insisting that one is French, or European, or simply a human being. While individual Bretons do not agree on all the same markers of Breton identity, it is nonetheless impossible to conclude from the work of Le Coadic, Favereau, Kuter and others that for Bretons today identity is constructed chiefly of 'invented' images based on a mythologized past projected into the present. Rather, in sifting through the evidence, Breton identity today appears, above all, to be based on a powerful sense of attachment to a physical territory and its looks, as well as a sense of sharing, however diffusely, in a way of life. These appear to be widespread features of identity which make Bretons feel distinctive within France and Europe.

Expressions of Breton identity through the EMSAV (the Breton movement)

Beginning in the early nineteenth century, intellectual and religious leaders in Brittany founded groups, associations, newspapers, literary circles and publishing houses to preserve and/or promote Breton culture, language and economic interests. A political arm was later added to this ensemble of activities, collectively referred to as the *emsav*, or Breton movement (Favereau 1993).

The establishment of scholarly and literary circles and academies and the propagation of Breton-language publications by the Catholic Church were manifestations of the first wave of the *emsav*. In 1898, a political organization was formed, *L'Union régionaliste bretonne* ('The Breton Regionalist Union'), which attempted economic and political reforms and advocated teaching Breton in the schools. In 1911 the first *Parti nationaliste breton* ('Breton Nationalist Party') would appear, a radical group that advocated severing all ties with France and reinstating Breton as the national language. The eruption of the first world war brought an end to these activities.

The second wave of the movement took shape after the war, with the founding in 1919 of a student organization called *Breiz Atao* ('Brittany Forever') that, looking to the Irish events of 1916 as a model, sought Breton autonomy. There were several other political groups organized during the interwar period, with separatist and sometimes fascist leanings that did not resonate with the general Breton public, particularly following the outbreak of WWII. Bretons massively joined the Resistance, though the much publicized efforts of a handful of Breton militants to collaborate with the Nazis in the hopes of establishing an independent state after the war received the lion's share of attention, creating a legacy of fear and distrust of Breton activism that lingers to this day. However, an important cultural initiative was launched during this same period, with the founding of the first truly literary journal (*Gwalarn*), inaugurating the renaissance of Breton-language literature.

The movement's third wave emerged after WWII, with the appearance of additional literary journals, folkloric festivals and musical groups. A non-partisan, broad-based organization, the *Comité d'étude et de liaison des intérêts bretons* (CELIB, 'Committee for the Study and Liaison of Breton Interests') aiming at the development of Brittany's economy was formed in 1950–51. This was eclipsed in 1956 by the more politically oriented *Mouvement pour l'organisation de la Bretagne* ('Movement for the Organization of Brittany') which called for greater decentralization in the management of the Breton economy (Keating 1985, p. 10); and a few years later the left-leaning *Union démocratique bretonne* ('Breton Democratic Union') a political party, was created. The UDB is still active and advocates more regional autonomy, even independence, and a federation of European regions. Along with similar groups with whom it has sometimes allied itself, however, it has not succeeded in attracting more than a tiny percentage of the regional vote (3 per cent in 1992: Favereau 1993, p. 79).

Without doubt, one of the great accomplishments of this last wave was the founding, in 1977, of the first successful bilingual (Breton/French) schools in Brittany. Called *Diwan* ('seed, sprout'), this pedagogical movement has evolved in 22 years from a single nursery-school classroom with five students to a network of 25 schools, from nursery to *lycée* level, teaching close to 1800 students within 20 years of its founding.[14] *Diwan* has often faced financial difficulties, but has succeeded in staying afloat, and in the 1980s it negotiated with the Ministry of Education for recognition and some monetary support for the salaries of their teachers.[15] In 1997, the first cohort of 12 young people entirely educated entirely within this bilingual system successfully passed their baccalaureate exams in Breton.

Breton opinion – in both Upper and Lower Brittany – is generally very favourable to this initiative, with one survey showing that 88 per cent of Bretons, whether or not they speak Breton, believe it should be maintained (Kergoat 1998, p. 420). For many, the language has high symbolic value as a feature of Breton identity. For example, one of Le Coadic's interviewees remarked that Breton, *'ça donne les couleurs de la Bretagne! Ça montre qu'on est là. Qu'on n'est pas en voie d'extinction!'* [that gives colour to Brittany! That shows that we exist. That we are not about to become extinct!] And another: *'Mais le Breton, ça serait un catastrophe s'il disparaissait!'* [But Breton, it would be a catastrophe if it disappeared!] (1998, p. 213). However, others express ambivalence: for example, one interviewee, while indicating a certain amount of admiration for the people who have worked for the *Diwan* schools, recoiled at the thought of sending his own children to one, stating '*Ça me laisse froid, ça ne me motive absolument pas*' [That leaves me cold, that absolutely does not motivate me] (ibid., p. 203). Another was of the opinion that '*Il ne faut pas rester une heure à apprendre, mais une petite demi-heure ou même cinq minutes suffisent à apprendre un truc en breton*' [You shouldn't spend an hour teaching it, but a half-hour or even five minutes will suffice to teach a thing or two in Breton] (ibid.).

Another area of movement promoting the language has been the establishment of a Breton presence in the broadcast media. During the early 1940s, the first Breton-language radio broadcasts were diffused in parts of Lower Brittany, but all this activity ceased in 1945. Very limited Breton-language broadcasting resumed in the 1950s, and gradually increased over following decades. At present there are 11 radio stations in Brittany, only two of them subsidized by the audio-visual licence fee; the others are private, most with broadcasting time limited to two or three hours per week. (Denez 1998, p. 30). Many of these stations can only be received within a restricted geographic range. Moreover, the proportion of Breton language to musical offerings is, generally speaking, low.

The situation for Breton television is weak, and has not changed much over two decades. The main station, broadcasting from Rennes, provides about 40 minutes weekly of Breton language programmes to eastern Brittany, and 65 minutes to western Brittany (Bro Nevez 1998, p. 3), generally broadcast on Sundays; while the Brest station offers Breton only five or six minutes daily (Denez 1998, p. 31). The lack of television programming for children and adolescents is problematic, and an area in need of development.

Bretons vis-à-vis Europe

Bretons at the turn of the twenty-first century incontestably feel part of the greater European complex of nations and regions. As they look around them, they see regions of comparable size with strong economies and ethno-linguistic identities actively participating in the life of the European Community; often cited in this connection are Catalonia, Bavaria, Flanders, Wales and Scotland. Many Bretons feel strongly that they have the means, and the right, to achieve equivalent standing within Europe. The vast majority of the Breton population appears to have no interest in seeking independence from France; but there is strong support for achieving greater regional autonomy within the state. This would afford Bretons a higher degree of local control of economic initiatives, commercial partnering and cultural exchanges with other European nations and regions, and would help effect the stabilization and nurturance of resources needed to promote employment, culture and education within Brittany.

Thus, it is interesting, if not especially surprising, to note that Brittany favoured the Maastricht Treaty of 1992, with about 60 per cent of Bretons voting affirmatively on this referendum concerning the encouragement of multi-faceted cooperation among European states. By contrast, France as a whole (along with Denmark), rejected the Treaty, with a negative vote of about 58 per cent. Favereau (1993, p. 139) interprets the Breton vote 'in favour of Europe' as a clear sign of Bretons' sense of openness to countries beyond France and an affirmation of their own feeling of identity, distinct from a French one.

Another issue of prominence within the European Union in recent years that has found wide support in Brittany is the adoption by the European Council in 1992 of the European Charter for Regional and Minority Languages, readied for ratification by member states in November 1994. France was very slow to respond, worrying that this charter, if ratified, would be in conflict with Article 2 of the Constitution in which it is stated that 'the language of the Republic is French'. After years of delay, the charter was at last signed by a French official in Budapest on 7 May 1999, thus, lending some additional legal protection for, and in principle, promotion of, regional and minority languages in France (of which there are at least 25). Ironically, within six weeks of signing, the French Constitutional Council ruled the charter contrary to fundamental [French] law, arguing that the Constitution would need to be revised to allow for the charter's full, legal ratification; this decision places the charter in a state of suspended animation (*Le Monde*, 19 juin, 1999). Disappointment, and no small measure of cynicism, has been the widespread reaction among linguistic and cultural activists in Brittany and elsewhere.

The future of the Breton language

It is estimated that 10 000 to 20 000 native speakers – older generations of Bretons – die each year, and they are not being replaced in comparable numbers of young Breton-speakers. With an approximate base of 240 000 regular speakers of the language (Broudic 1999), it requires little reflection to realize that the language is unlikely to perpetuate itself indefinitely. The *neo-bretonnants* ('new Breton speakers') coming through the *Diwan* schools and other bilingual programmes (with about 4000 enrolled each year) will help dampen the loss, but there are real questions surrounding these cohorts of speakers: how fluent are they in Breton, what sort of Breton do they speak, and with whom will they speak it outside of the school premises? – an ironic inversion of the nineteenth century French-in-the-school, Breton-elsewhere scene.

Some young people trained in the school/literary version of the language may establish Breton-speaking households and families, and contribute to the intergenerational transmission of the language. But the home domain, though crucial for a language, is an insufficient basis for its full flourishing. At present, French is indisputably the dominant language in nearly aspect of public life in Brittany, in spite of recent symbolic bows to Breton in the form of bilingual signage for the names of cities, towns, rivers and so on, and in the presence, though limited, of Breton in the broadcast media. There is a growing number of writers and publishers of Breton-language materials, but the readership remains diminutive; and the Breton-language film industry is in its infancy. On the other hand, Breton music – pipe bands and other instrumental ensembles, a traditional vocal genre called *kan ha diskan*, dance music, jazz and rock (often with Breton lyrics) – has experienced a remarkable growth over the past 20 years, and is a source of pleasure and a means of asserting Breton identity for young people in particular. Popular music may be the single most effective means of attracting children and young adults to the language and to inspire in them a desire to learn it. This is important for, as Broudic (1999, p. 126) observes, reversing the effects of steady language loss that is taking place in Brittany will require two things: (1) a considerable growth in the number of individuals who learn Breton as a second language; and (2) effective use of the language in society by those who do learn it.

Conclusions

I opened this chapter with Lebesque's question as to how one can be Breton. The answer is a complex one, as he demonstrated in his book, and as I have further explored in this chapter. Breton identity is, certainly, as Lebesque holds, a question of consciousness and of will. He does not insist on the Breton language as part of this consciousness, although he is in favour of its perpetuation and instruction. Other Breton intellectuals and activists do insist: Le Gars (1998), for example, calls for a massive re-Bretonization of both Upper and Lower Brittany;

while the thoughts of ordinary people – such as are found in Le Coadic's interviews, and such as I have encountered in my own field work in Brittany – are mixed on this matter. Some look to Ireland as a model of an independent nation-state, with a strong Celtic culture, in which the traditional Gaelic language has largely been supplanted by English, although enjoying official status. Others use terms such as 'catastrophic' were the language to disappear.

Late twentieth century Bretons have mainly left behind the negative attitudes that earlier generations expressed about their traditional tongue, attitudes that were common when the majority of the population still spoke it. Now that the long-term survival of Breton is in question, it is perhaps easier to feel affection and nostalgia for it. But its contribution at present to the formation of Bretons' sense of identity is variable, not categorical. Bretons have additional features by which they identify themselves and feel distinctive, and proud, vis-à-vis other cultural minorities in France, and in Europe. There is a slogan *Hep brezhoneg, Breizh ebet* ('Without Breton, there is no Brittany') that was much in evidence in the 1970s in Brittany. Although it is clear that in the late 1990s many Bretons did still attach much symbolic value to the Breton language, the evidence suggests that they have additional cultural and economic resources, as well as special geographic/ territorial ones, with which to assert and perpetuate a distinctive identity in the twenty-first century.

Notes

1. According to Weber (1991, p. 57), this way of describing France did not become common until the 1960s; he dates the earliest 'positive mention of France's hexagonal shape' to 1894.
2. See Giot (1999) for an alternative account.
3. Loître-Atlantique was administratively severed from the other four departments during the Occupation (in 1941) and has never been reunited.
4. Le Gars (1998, p. 22) puts a another spin on this distinction, suggesting that the mildly pejorative Upper/Lower duality stems from a centrist perception that the portion of the peninsula that is closer to Paris and is francophone is superior (higher) to the inferior (lower) portion that is more distant and non-French speaking. 'Eastern Brittany' and 'Western Brittany' are more neutral terms, but the older labels are still commonly used.
5. Durand (1996, p. 78) notes a parallel phenomenon among the fifteenth-century 'ruling élite in the south of France [who] embraced the language of the French kings – a move which gave it access to powerful social, cultural and economic networks'.

6. There are no solid census data regarding numbers of Breton or other minority language speakers in France, and the calculations that have been made are, in effect, 'guestimates'. F. Broudic in 1997 carried out one of the most thorough surveys to date. See his 1995 dissertation for a thorough assessment of prior attempts to calculate the number of Breton speakers; he is particularly critical of the figure of 1.3 million cited above for the late nineteenth century, proposed by the folklorist Paul Sébillot (1886). His calculations were evidently filled with errors (Broudic 1995, pp. 30–1).

7. In 1880 the rector of Rennes wrote 'Frenchify Brittany as promptly as possible ...; integrate western Brittany with the rest of France', to be accomplished chiefly through schooling (Weber 1976, p. 100).

8. Thus it is not surprising that there should be evidence of what Jones (1976) calls 'an incipient nationalism' in certain fourteenth century Breton writers. For example, the secretary and biographer of the Breton Duke John IV (who had sworn fealty to the French king), wrote that:

   the duke was not the liege man of the king of France; Brittany and France were two separate entities and there was little respect amongst the Bretons for the French, an effeminate race of men with forked beards. ... (p. 144)

9. The first dictionary, a trilingual Breton–Latin–French work called *Le Catholicon*, appeared as a manuscript in 1464 and then as the first incunable in Breton in 1499; it was intended for Breton-speaking clergy. The missionizing priest Julien Manoir published the first Breton grammar, *Le Sacré College de Jésus* ('Sacred College of Jesus') in 1659, which also included a dictionary (Hardie 1948, pp. 8–9).

10. A common, though not universally applied, method of enforcing French on school premises was the so-called *symbole* ('symbol') or *vache* ('cow'). Laîné (1992, p. 67) says that this practice was found scattered throughout Europe, but was especially prevalent in France, and consisted in stigmatizing a youngster caught speaking Breton (or other non-authorized language) by forcing the child to display some visible sign of his/her shame. The child so marked could only be relieved of this humiliation by catching a schoolmate speaking the forbidden language and thus passing the *symbole* on to another. The *symbole* varied locally, but in Brittany it was often a wooden shoe. Weber remarks that, ironically, this punishment came through the Jesuits, who had used it to enforce the speaking of Latin in favour of French (1976, p. 313).

11. Kergoat maintains that *'"dans sa tête" le Breton avait déjà changé de langue en 1950'* [in his head, the Breton had already changed languages in 1950] (1999, p. 417).

12. As Renan deftly put it: 'Forgetting history, or even getting history wrong are an essential factor in the formation of a nation, which is why the progress of historical studies is often dangerous to a nationality' (quoted in Hobsbawm 1992, p. 3).

13. He also conducted a number of 'exploratory interviews' in advance of the 46, with well-known Breton intellectuals, writers, and musicians in order to draw out salient issues and to garner the perspectives of Bretons who were likely to have given serious thought to the issue of Breton identity.

14. According to Diwan's website data, there were 1753 students enrolled for the 1997–98 academic year.
15. The history of this pedagogical movement is far more complex, and politically charged, than can be covered here. The interested reader will find an excellent account of the initiative's first two decades in Perazzi (1998).

Bibliography

Abalain, H. *Histoire de la langue bretonne*. (Luçon: Editions J.-P. Gisserot, 1995).

Anderson, B.R. *Imagined Communities; Reflections on the Origins and Spread of Nationalism* (London: Verso, 1983).

Barbour, S., 'Language and National Identity in Europe; Theoretical and Practical Problems', In C. Hoffmann, ed., *Language, Culture and Communication in Contemporary Europe* (Philadelphia: Multilingual Matters, 1996), pp. 28–45.

Bro Nevez 'Breton Language Radio' 65 (1998), 3.

Broudic, F. *La pratique du breton de l'ancien régime à nos jours* (Rennes: Presses universitaires de Rennes, 1995).

Broudic, F. *Qui parle breton aujourd'hui? Qui le parlera demain?* (Brest: Brud Nevez, 1999).

Chapman, M. *The Celts. The Construction of a Myth* (New York: St. Martin's Press – now Palgrave, 1992).

Chapman, M. McDonald, M. and Tonkin, E. 'Introduction', in E. Tonkin, M. McDonald and M. Chapman, eds, *History and Ethnicity* (New York: London, 1989), pp. 1–21.

Denez, P. *Brittany. A Language in Search of a Future* (Brussels: European Bureau for Lesser Used Languages, 1998).

Dietler, M. '*Our Ancestors the Gauls*: Archaeology, Ethnic Nationalism and the Manipulation of Celtic Identity in Modern Europe', *American Anthropologist*, 96 (1994), 584–605.

Durand, J., 'Linguistic Purification, the French Nation-State and the Linguist', in C. Hoffmann, ed., *Language, Culture and Communication in Contemporary Europe* (Philadelphia: Multilingual Matters, 1996), pp. 75–92.

Favereau, F. *Bretagne contemporaine. Langue, culture, identité* (Morlaix: Skol Vreizh, 1993).

Giot, P.-R., 'La genèse des mythes autour du fait de l'arrivé des Bretons en Armorique' in H. ar Bihan, ed., *Breizh ha Poploù Europa/Bretagne et Peuples d'Europe* (Sant-Tonan: Klask, 1999), pp. 283–307.

Gourvil, F. *Langue et littérature bretonnes* (Paris: Presses universitaires de France, 1968).

Hardie, D.W.F. *A Handbook of Modern Breton (Armorican)* (Cardiff: University of Wales Press, 1948).

Hechter, M. *Internal Colonialism: the Celtic Fringe in British National Development, 1536–1966* (Berkeley: University of California Press, 1975).

Hobsbawm, E. 'Introduction: Inventing Traditions', in E. Hobsbawm and T. Ranger, eds, *The Invention of Tradition* (New York: Cambridge University Press, 1983), pp. 1–14.

Hobsbawm, E., 'Ethnicity and Nationalism in Europe Today', *Anthropology Today*, 8 (1992), 3–8.

Jones, M. *'Mon Pais et ma Nation*: Breton Identity in the Fourteenth Century', in C.T. Allmand, ed., *War, Literature and Politics in the Late Middle Ages* (Liverpool: Liverpool University Press, 1976), pp. 144–68.

Keating, M., 'The Rise and Decline of Micronationalism in Mainland France', *Political Studies*, XXXIII (1985), 1–18.

Kergoat, L., 'Une Bretagne en quête de'identité: la relation à la langue', In H. ar Bihan, ed., *Breizh ha Poploù Europa/Bretagne et Peuples d'Europe* (Sant-Tonan: Klask, 1999), pp. 393–413.

Kuter, L., 'Labeling people: Who are the Bretons?', *Anthropological Quarterly*, 58 (1985), 13–29.

Laîné, N. *Le droit à la parole* (Rennes: Terre de Brume, 1992).

Lebesque, M. *Comment peut-on être breton? Essai sur la démocratie française* (Paris: Seuil, 1970).

Le Coadic, R. *L'identité bretonne* (Rennes: Terre de Brume, 1998).

Le Gars, A. *Les Bretons par eux-mêmes* (Kergleuz: An Here, 1998).

Le Monde, 'M. Jospin et M. Chirac pris dans la polémique sur les langues régionales', 19 juin (1999), 8.

McDonald, M. *'We are not French!' Language, Culture and Identity in Brittany* (New York: Routledge, 1989).

Maynard, D. 'Rurality, Rusticity, and Contested Identity Politics in Brittany', in B. Ching and G.W. Creed, eds, *Knowing Your Place. Rural Identity and Cultural Hierarchy* (New York: Routledge, 1997), pp. 195–218.

Perazzi, J.-C. *Diwan. Vingt ans d'enthousiasme, de doute et d'espoir* (Spézet: Coop Breizh, 1998).

Rannou, P. 'Littérature et bretonnité. Premiere partie' *Le Peuple Breton*, 278 (1987), 13–15.

Reece, J.E. *The Bretons against France. Ethnic, Minority Nationalism in Twentieth-Century Brittany* (Chapel Hill: The University of North Carolina Press, 1977).

Smith, A. *The Ethnic Revival* (New York: Cambridge University Press, 1981).

Timm, L.A. 'Modernization and Language Shift: the Case of Brittany, *Anthropological Linguistics*, 15 (1973): 281–98.

Timm, L.A., 'Against All Odds: Language Promotion Efforts in Brittany', in J.N. Jørgensen, *et al.*, eds, *Bilingualism in School and Society* (Philadelphia: Multilingual Matters, 1988), pp. 19–32.

Weber, E. *Peasants into Frenchmen. The Modernization of Rural France, 1870–1914* (Stanford: Stanford University Press, 1976).

Weber, E. *My France. Politics, Culture, Myth* (Cambridge, Mass.: Belknap Press, 1991).

Zernatto, G., 'Nation: The History of a Word', *Review of Politics*, 6 (1944), 351–66.

7
When Language Does Not Matter: Regional Identity Formation in Northern Italy

Jaro Stacul

Introduction[1]

The recent political transformations in Eastern Europe (not to mention the conflict in Kosovo) and the rise of regionalist movements in the EU have raised the issue of linguistic identity dramatically at a time when the legitimacy of the centralized nation-state is being challenged, even in nation-states in which language has never emerged as a problem. The almost symbiotic relationship between language and nationalism is far from being a new phenomenon: a standard criterion of what constitutes a nation with a claim to self-determination is ethnic-linguistic (Hobsbawm 1992, p. 3), and from its modern inception in the late eighteenth century nationalism was inextricably bound up with language (Kedourie 1961, p. 71).

The role of language in the forging of national identity figures centrally in the work of Anthony Smith (1986). Anderson (1991) too recognizes the conjunction of language and nation-state in the modern world. Ideally, for the construction of a nation-state to be successful, political and linguistic boundaries should be coterminous (Gellner 1983), and it is especially under changing political circumstances that language is very likely to become problematic. Language was a crucial factor for national identity formation in Eastern Europe after the break-up of nation-states such as the USSR and Yugoslavia: nowadays, for example, to be considered a full Estonian citizen, people have to give evidence that they can speak Estonian fluently. Similarly, various studies (for example, Macdonald 1997, McDonald 1989) have shown that what unites most of the autonomist and separatist movements in Western Europe (Basque, Breton, Scottish, Welsh and others) is their stress on language as a distinctive factor.

However, while a currently spoken language, such as Basque, may act as a marker of national identity, other languages, such as Irish, Breton or Occitan, have to be revitalized or virtually invented. O'Reilly (1998, p. 46) has observed that for the majority of the people in Northern Ireland, Irish ceased to be spoken as a language of everyday communication long before partition, and now it is imbued with symbolic importance associated with Irish nationalism. Breton identity was built upon the imposition of a 'standard' language that the people in question found difficult to speak, which nonetheless was useful for the construction of a distinct 'cultural identity' (McDonald 1989, pp. 162–71). Similarly, Occitan is a language that nobody speaks, because it is the sum of a number of different dialects, but it was functional to the creation of an imagined 'Occitanie' (Bourdieu 1991, p. 223). In these cases, language operates as a symbol, and remains of value only in the symbolic sense (Edwards 1985, p. 18). So, whether 'authentic', 'invented' or 'revitalized', language may play a crucial role in the definition of an 'imagined community' such as a region or a nation-state.

Other scholars, although pointing to the significant role of language itself, do not necessarily see it as a decisive factor in national identity formation: for Renan (1882/1947), for example, language was not essential for nationalism; for Edwards (1985, p. 22) it is not even important for identity maintenance. Hobsbawm (1990, p. 154) has argued that national languages are '... almost always semi-artificial constructs and occasionally ... virtually invented'. As the same author observes (1990, p. 170), although the significance of linguistic identity cannot be denied, neither language nor ethnicity are always essential to nationalism (Hobsbawm 1992, p. 4), and in the future history will have to take into account the development of a world which cannot be contained within the limits of nations defined economically or linguistically (Hobsbawm 1990, p. 181).

While the significance of language in the forging of national or regional identity might seem obvious in contexts such as the Basque country, Brittany, Corsica, Scotland or Wales, it is not always so in areas in which the success of regionalist parties largely derives from their capacity to appeal to themes already existent in local 'culture', which do not necessarily include language. In addition, in some cases, the regional autonomy that such movements champion is predicated more upon affluence than upon a 'cultural' identity (Harvie 1994, p. 5). As Wilson has observed (1996, p. 213), the new definition of border in a 'Europe without frontiers' makes the notion of borders as fluid as a 'Europe of the regions'.

One of the issues that the language question raises, at least in contemporary Western Europe, is its relationship with an increasingly integrated European Union in which national boundaries are declining in significance: the European Union itself is characterized by the apparent contradiction between economic unification and linguistic autonomy. Although it has been suggested that a European Union will not end the historic identities of the *ethnies* and nations of Europe (Smith 1996, p. 125; see also Friedman 1994, p. 218), the role of language remains problematic. In fact the EEC Treaty does not contain any rules relating to language use, and does not affect the linguistic policies of the member states (De Witte 1993, p. 156): languages and 'cultures' have to be preserved, but borders can be crossed freely, and people increasingly define themselves in terms of groups and communities that may be supra-national (Miller 1995, p. 156). So, while the ethnolinguistic identities just mentioned are consistent with the Wilsonian doctrine one language = one territory, it may be asked whether the same applies to the new Europe, whose 'transnational' character contrasts sharply with that before European economic integration.

Regional identity in Northern Italy

In the remainder of this chapter I will try to provide at least a partial answer to the questions raised above by drawing on ethnographic information collected in northern Italy, in the Trentino province, between 1995 and 1996. Northern Italy lends itself particularly well to an exploration of the redefinition of national identity because of the political changes of the early 1990s which paved the way for the advent of autonomist and regionalist political movements, particularly the *Lega Nord*/Northern League. Such a movement had in its agenda the transformation of Italy into a federal state and, for some time, even the division between the wealthy North and the poorer South of the country. Central to its rhetoric was stress on local history and traditions, opposition to state influence, and the idea that northern Italy partakes of a 'central European' culture as opposed to a 'Mediterranean' one.[2]

Perhaps one of the most intriguing aspects of the Northern League's ideology, particularly in the early 1990s, was that the northern Italian identity it championed was not built on linguistic differences: the movement could not appeal to a distinct language as a marker of identification, because northern Italy (not to mention Lombardy, where the movement was established) includes provinces speaking very different dialects (Strassoldo 1996, p. 82), and the language of the North is not different from that spoken in Rome.

One of the core-values of the Northern League's ideology was Europeanism. In more recent years this has been neglected (Strassoldo 1996, p. 83). However, it remained prominent in the agenda of other autonomist movements elsewhere in northern Italy. The mountainous Trentino province is a case in point: it forms an autonomous region together with the German-speaking South Tyrol, with which it shares a common history. It was one of the southernmost administrative units of the Austro-Hungarian empire until its disintegration in 1918, even though Italian (along with Italian dialects) is the main language used in communication.

The ascendancy of regionalist movements in that area cannot be understood unless it is borne in mind that, given the significant degree of autonomy of the province, in most of Trentino the state does not have the same significance that it has in other Italian regions. It must also be stressed that the city of Trent, where most of the national offices in the province are based, is far away from the Alpine valleys where most of the Trentine population lives. It is the municipality (*comune*) and the province (*provincia*), rather than the state, that loom largest in the lives of most of the inhabitants of Trentino. The over-whelming majority of the public offices are owned by the *provincia* itself, whose symbol (an eagle) can be noticed in almost every corner of the provincial territory. The limited presence of the state apparatus at the local level has certainly influenced the people's 'sense of place'. Local particularism in the field of law has also played an important part, given that the province, together with South Tyrol, has retained some laws that date from Austro-Hungarian times, especially with regard to the use of land and natural resources.

It is outside the scope of the present chapter to explore the political history of Trentino in detail, so I will confine myself to an analysis of the relationship between language and regional identity. In the eighteenth century there was little dispute about what part of the region was Italian and what was German: the terms were those defined in cultural linguistic terms, and began to assume political importance in the nineteenth century (Levy 1988, p. 13). In spite of the fact that Trentino was under Austro-Hungarian sovereignty, there was no attempt to Germanize all aspects of life in the lands of the Empire, and the Habsburgs were quite willing to see children educated in their own language (Levy 1988, p. 141). It should also be noted that there was a discrepancy between linguistic identity and linguistic classification: the Austrian census of 1910, for example, classified population by language habitually spoken, not by mother tongue. As a consequence, people with German as mother tongue could be classified as Italian, and people with Italian as mother tongue could be classified as German (Cole and Wolf 1974, p. 289). This had the effect of making the categories 'Italian' and 'Austrian' less fixed than might be thought, and in all likelihood has affected the way people perceive such categories nowadays, as will be seen later on in this chapter.

On the eve of the Great War the border between Trentino and South Tyrol was clearly marked, the former being overwhelmingly populated by Italian speakers, the latter by German speakers. With the end of the Great War the two provinces were annexed to the Italian Kingdom. However, while Trentino shared with Italy at least a language, the same did not apply to the other province, and especially after the end of the Great War there was a tendency to stress the 'Italian' character of Trentino, as opposed to the German-speaking South Tyrol (Poppi 1991; Sanguanini 1992, p. 149).

The demise of the Fascist regime and the end of the Second World War led Italy and Austria to a political settlement which involved granting Trentino, and particularly South Tyrol, autonomy. In fact the agreement was designed to ensure that the cultural, economic and social development of the South Tyroleans lay in Italian hands (Alcock 1996, p. 73). So, even in the aftermath of the last world conflict, the differentiation between the two provinces remained primarily linguistic, and much of the way society was organized in South Tyrol depended on a declaration relating to ethnic identity.

Despite the fact that in nationalist discourse Trentino was presented as an 'Italian' province, at the local level 'Italianness' did not necessarily convey ideas of distinctiveness vis-à-vis South Tyrol. This is suggested by the fact that before the autonomy agreement a short-lived protest movement all over Trentino, the Association for the Study of Regional Autonomy (ASAR), asked for autonomy and unity for the two provinces. On 20 April 1947, a huge crowd gathered in the main square of the city of Trent to assert self-determination, and many of the participants carried a banner bearing the heading 'I am Austrian' (in Italian) in spite of the fact that in Trentino German is not used in everyday communication. At that time the idea of unity of the two provinces was so powerful that it was proposed that it would be better for the whole region to be annexed by Austria rather than have them separated (Alcock 1970, p. 90).

A 'European' region?

The situation so far described has changed with the process of Western European economic and political integration. National boundaries were no longer considered as important as they used to be, and the rise of regionalism challenged one of the principles central to the definition of the nation-state, that of cultural uniformity. In 1992, with the Maastricht Treaty, it was admitted that regions had a place in the construction of Europe, and the Italian political crisis of the early 1990s paved the way for the advent of the Northern League and the Trentine-Tyrolean Autonomist Party (PATT), which made big inroads in Trentino. Another important change occurred in 1992, when it was admitted that the Italians residing in South Tyrol could call themselves South Tyroleans (Luverà 1996, p. 33), even those who could not speak German. Until the early 1990s, being able to speak German and the local German dialects was central to the definition of who was a South Tyrolean; in 1992, however, such a notion involved the acknowledgement of the coexistence of two ethnic groups: anybody who lives in South Tyrol is South Tyrolean, irrespective of the ethnic group they belong to.

The political and economic crisis in Italy of the early 1990s entailed the risk, for Trentino, of losing the status of special autonomous province from which it had so far benefited. One of the ways in which Trentino could cope with this situation was by establishing an Autonomous European Region of Tyrol, or Euregio, encompassing Trentino itself, South Tyrol, and the Austrian region of Tyrol, and by stressing distinctiveness vis-à-vis the Italian nation-state – otherwise its likely fate was to become an ordinary Italian region (Alcock 1996, p. 83).

Probably the most intriguing aspect of this unusual political situation was the form that the construction of regional identity took: on the one hand the necessity to preserve the autonomy granted from the national government pushed Trentino to assert its cultural distinctiveness; on the other, the appeal that the concept of 'Europe' had with European integration meant that Europe itself could act as a tool to legitimate self-determination. As has been observed (Shore and Black 1994, pp. 291–4), this was a consequence of the European Union's policy aimed at promoting local identities and European regions, which can also bring about renewed stress on regional identity and the erosion of national consensus.

The attempt to establish an Autonomous European Region was accompanied by an attempt to define a 'regional', 'local' history and culture. The construction of a past, by its very nature, is a project that selectively organizes events in a relation of continuity with a contemporary subject (Friedman 1992, p. 837): one possible horizon within which a regional history could be constructed was that of pre-1918 Trentino, when the province was part of a larger Austrian region of Tyrol (Alcock 1996, p. 83). In a sense, the paradoxical aspect was that the political and cultural distinctiveness of Trentino vis-à-vis the nation-state was not so much predicated upon the existence of a putative authentic Trentine culture, as on common culture and unbroken history with the neighbouring German-speaking regions. This was all the more unusual allowing for the fact that, as already noted, from the late nineteenth century until recently, Trentino was distinguished from South Tyrol on the grounds that it was an Italian region.

Central to the rhetoric of politicians was the prominence given to the region (both Trentino and a would-be Euregio) as a constituent part of a 'Europe' in which national boundaries have less significance. Being part of 'Europe' entailed looking beyond national frontiers. In fact this idea of 'Europe' replicates a feature of separatist claims, notably the distinction between 'Europeans' as 'modern', 'prosperous', 'culturally distinct northerners' as opposed to the allegedly 'backward', 'lazy', 'subsidized' Mediterranean southerners (Judt 1997, p. 114). 'Europe' was pointed to as the repository of the values which were seen as lacking in a nation-state, such as Italy, which was experiencing a political crisis. So, the obvious link between Trentino and a more prosperous and politically stable 'Europe' was a common history with Tyrol.

The other point stressed by party spokesmen (not to mention academic historians) was that of autonomy: Trentino is an autonomous province, and this autonomy has historical foundations. In the politicians' rhetoric the origin of autonomy could be found in the rural past, as epitomized by the fact that local people have always had direct control over land. More importantly, the fact that the provincial territory has not suffered from environmental degradation was pointed to as a positive result of this (Coppola 1994, p. 135).

An almost immediate effect of this political propaganda was that some of the national symbols that had so far been ascribed to a 'South Tyrolean tradition' were borrowed on the grounds that Trentino too partook of the same 'tradition'. So, for example, the Austro-Hungarian emperor, Franz Josef, became the 'Emperor of Trentino'; Andreas Hofer, the innkeeper who led a rebellion of Trentine and South Tyrolean peasants against Napoleon in the early nineteenth century, was pointed to as the incarnation of Trentine and South Tyrolean liberty. What these two political leaders have in common is that they symbolized the unity of the two ethnic groups when both Trentino and South Tyrol were under Austrian sovereignty: they stressed the 'multicultural' character of the province. Both the emperor and Andreas Hofer figure prominently in Trentine history, but they had until recently been treated as national symbols of Tyrol or Austria, not of the Italian-speaking Trentino.

It is not purely coincidence that many of the Trentini who attended the huge gathering of Trentine autonomists in November 1994, by the village of Borghetto at the southern border between Trentino and Veneto, wore the clothes that are seen as ethnic symbols of South Tyrol. Perhaps the most noticeable 'borrowing' was the establishment, in Trentino, of groups of *Schützen*, the civil militia identified by public opinion at large with Tyrolean nationalism. Although there was awareness that such groups were in fact expression of another 'culture', they were considered useful to create traditions in places, such as Alpine villages, where local traditions were fast disappearing.

An underlying aspect of this 'appropriation' was that in Trentino a 'Tyrolean' or 'Austrian' culture did not include language: while Gaelic or Breton may be given political expression, the same does not apply to the multiplicity of dialects spoken in Trentino. This raises the issue of why the idea that Trentino shares a 'culture' with Tyrol and Austria achieved considerable appeal even though German is not spoken. That the Tyrolean legacy still plays a significant role there is a truism. What should be borne in mind is that ideologies are not necessarily imposed: if they achieve their appeal, it is because they accommodate themselves to local-level discourses (Sahlins 1989, p. 8). As far as the area studied is concerned, the success that the idea of a European region enjoyed can hardly be accounted for without allowing for the meanings attached by the people involved to categories such as 'Italian' and 'Austrian'. This aspect is explored in the following section.

Local identity and language

In all likelihood the development of state administration in Trentino (both the Austro-Hungarian and the Italian one) played a decisive role in devaluing dialects and establishing a hierarchy of linguistic practices (see, for example, Bourdieu 1991, p. 49). The many dialects of Trentino could hardly aspire to the same status that the Italian language has. In spite of this, the fact that language does not now figure prominently in the politicians' construction of regional identity should not blind us to the fact that language itself, and especially dialects, may be central to the definition of who is a villager and who is not.

It must be noted that there is no regional dialect that is spoken throughout the Trentine territory: each Alpine valley is characterized by its own Italian dialect,[3] though the Ladin areas and the German linguistic islands are exceptions. What is referred to as the Trentine dialect is in fact that spoken in the city of Trent and its environs. In the western part of the province most of the inhabitants speak a Lombard dialect, whereas in the opposite part a variant of Venetic is used in everyday communication. Despite the variety of dialects, and their similarity to those of the surrounding Italian-speaking regions, there seems to be a widespread conviction that sharing a common history with Trentini is more important than sharing dialects with Veneti or Lombards who have a different history. It appears that regional identity in Trentino identity takes little or no account of dialects.

So, the fact that the same dialect is spoken across the regional border is not used, at the local level, to establish a relation of cultural continuity is significant: one calls oneself Trentine even though one speaks a Lombard or Venetic dialect. A dialect does not define a shared identity if spoken outside Trentino. In all likelihood, the fact that the province was for centuries a political entity distinct from the nearby Italian-speaking regions, and acted as a sort of buffer zone between northern and southern Europe, legitimated the idea that being Trentine mainly entails membership of a territorial unit.

These issues were clearly evident in the course of the fieldwork I conducted between 1995 and 1996 in the Vanoi valley, one of the easternmost municipalities of the province, in which both the Northern League and the Trentine-Tyrolean Autonomist Party made big inroads in the early 1990s. It is one of the largest *comuni* (communes) of Trentino, although its population has dropped during the last few decades. It lies close to the administrative boundary with the Veneto region, and has a population of scarcely 1700 inhabitants. Until the 1960s, local people lived by a combination of agriculture, forestry and animal husbandry. With the demise of agro-pastoral economy, the valley has become depopulated. In the valley much of the present-day population consists of the retired or manual workers in the local sawmill. Locals still have direct control over land, even though a substantial part of it has been bought by city dwellers who occasionally come there on vacation. At present the valley is dependent on outside capital and subsidies from the provincial government.

Because the area lies by the regional border, issues of regional and local identity inevitably come to the fore. However, while language is not used to establish a cultural continuity with the rest of Trentino, it is central to the definition of village identity. All the people of the Vanoi valley I have come across, irrespective of age and sex, are keen to distinguish the dialect and accent of their own village from that of the more prosperous nearby valleys. This sentiment is associated with the idea of 'community', it is invested with the sentiment attached to kinship and friendship, and at the local level it is looked upon as a 'language' in its own terms.

The role of elites in encouraging the use of dialects is worth mentioning: in the Vanoi valley and in the nearby municipalities there are people who write poetry in the local dialect. Until recently, local schoolteachers used to teach their pupils about local traditions and dialect: pupils were often allocated the task of collecting information about the dialectal names of agricultural implements, trees, flowers, animals and so on in order to become aware of the specificity of the local dialect. Nowadays, emphasis on the local idiom also reflects a concern with the disappearance of local traditions in the face of 'modernity' as a result of depopulation. There is a widespread conviction that fewer and fewer people in the valley are able to speak the dialect of 'the old days', that TV and newspapers are imposing a language villagers are not yet completely familiar with – although it can be understood.

That elites can promote the use of local dialects should not blind us to the fact that social actors may also be sensitive to the relevance of local idioms irrespective of outside forces. So, the idea of 'purity', in relation to the local dialect, becomes an object of debate when the local dialect itself is compared to that of a nearby municipality or village, even though this forms part of the same province. As one of my informants said, 'They [the inhabitants of the adjacent municipality] are of another "race", ... it is an imported "race", a "race" of Turks, Slavs, and Sardinians. ... They speak a different dialect, nobody here speaks like that.' They are referred to as '... a bunch of immigrants who speak an incomprehensible mixture of dialects that nobody understands'. So, the 'pure' dialect of the village is opposed to the mixture of dialects spoken a few miles away, which is used, in local discourse, to cast the people of that village as 'matter out of place', in Douglas's terms (1966). The idea of 'purity' of the local dialect was also stressed by the retired schoolteacher of the village of Caoria who, in the course of a conversation, said that the inhabitants of a hamlet across the regional border speak a 'perfect Caorian'; in saying so, he implied that it is not Caorians who speak the dialect of the nearby province, but it is the other way round. Similarly, during my fieldwork, a girl from a nearby village in the same valley came to live in Caoria with her relatives. One day, on a visit to her aunt, she was jokingly advised to adopt Caorian as the dialect of conversation, even though the idiom used in everyday communication in the other village is virtually identical to that of Caoria. Taking a hint from Heady's Friulian case study (1999, p. 212), it may be suggested that pride in the specificity of the Caorian dialect is a way of asserting the superiority of the local community on segmentary rivals such as neighbouring villages.

We and 'the 'Italians'

While the idea of 'purity' of the local dialect is used to define who is a villager and who is not, in the area studied, local identity may also take on an 'ethnic' flavour. This is suggested by the fact that the term used to address Italians from outside Trentino is *taliáni* ('Italians'), even though Caorians speak the local Italian dialect as mother tongue. An analysis of the way the term is used shows that it has various connotations. In local discourse, Italy includes the national territory south of the regional border. The statement *andòn in Italia* ('let us go to Italy') is often used by villagers when going shopping to the nearby Veneto region. This is central to an understanding of local identity: pre-1918 national boundaries, North and South, Europe and the Mediterranean, become lines of demarcation between 'we' and the 'Italians', between who is 'inside' and who is 'outside', and serve to construct difference.

One of the favourite topics of conversation of the local people, men and women alike, is that of the 'Italians' who visit the valley in the summertime. Those who fish around the village without permission, for instance, are always referred to as 'Italians'. This also applies to the people who go picking up mushrooms and berries that 'rightfully' belong to the community. In a sense, it may be suggested that 'Italians' are ascribed the same 'intrusive' behavioural character that in local discourse is considered typical of the nation-state. Villagers expressed on several occasions the view that 'Italians' cannot be trusted, as epitomized by the statement 'Italians are good, but are also thieves' (*talián l'e bon, ma ladro*).

However, while avoiding becoming an 'Italian' and adopting 'Italian' customs are necessary to keep membership of the community, at the same time merging into a wider population is perceived as a condition for economic success. The son of the late mayor of the municipality, for example, is one of the largest landowners of Caoria. Some of my informants argue that his being half (or the 'typical') 'Italian' has been a decisive factor, as his mother came from outside Trentino. Villagers' ideas about him, in this case, seem to associate Italianness and village-ness with 'class': there is a widespread conviction, in the village, that this man became wealthy because he is an 'Italian'. The association of Italianness with 'wealth' and of villageness with 'poverty' seems to evoke the image of a village as a 'social class' that ideally reproduces itself over time: so, if the village is 'poor', then one has to go out of the community and turn 'Italian' in order to enrich oneself. The fact that this man is referred to as 'Italian' is also associated with his enterpris-ing character and with his ability to appropriate a huge amount of land in and around Caoria at the expense of some co-villagers; so, his being labelled 'Italian' may also be accounted for by his having behaved like an 'intrusive stranger', a characteristic that in local discourse is often ascribed to a putative impersonal and exploitative state.

So, on the one hand, being addressed as an 'Italian' may be deroga-tory; on the other, it is an identity that certain people in the valley endeavour to achieve. However, 'Italy' also conveys ideas of moral cor-ruption owing to the political crisis that the country was experiencing at that time. So, for example, those who live and work across the regional border are referred to as 'Italians' even though the dialect they speak is the same. 'Italian' conveys ideas about the place where one lives. Ideally, any villager can turn 'Italian' if he or she goes to live in other Italian regions: in local discourse 'Italianness' has little to do with language.

Nowadays, Italian is the language of modern economy, of bureau-cracy, of TV, of newspapers. Many of the villagers I interacted with during my fieldwork said that although in everyday life dialect is used more often than Italian, they find it difficult to write in the local dialect, given that Italian is the language of compulsory primary educa-tion. In the valley, it is the younger generation, those of school age, who can speak Italian correctly and shift from the local dialect to the national language with very little or no difficulty. Although there is an almost shared conviction that it is necessary to turn 'Italian' in order to be able to deal with the government and be familiar with a bureau-cratic language, there is also awareness that the Italian spoken in the valley is that of the 'mountain people': there are various stories about Caorians who used to pride themselves on their ability to speak a correct Italian, but ended up mixing Italian and dialectal expressions, much to the amusement of their co-villagers. In other words, to be a Caorian and an Italian citizen at the same time is also to have a marginal Italian identity.

If speaking Italian or Italian dialects does not establish a relationship of cultural continuity between Trentino and the rest of Italy, then, how do villagers define themselves in relation to non-Trentini? The fact that the province was under Austrian sovereignty for centuries is often used, in local discourse, to stress similarity with the German speakers of South Tyrol or the Austrian Tyrol, and difference vis-à-vis the 'Italians' of the nearby Veneto region. All my informants, irrespective of age and gender, are well aware of the fact that they are not Austrians, for they have never spoken German, nor has German ever become the official language in the valley; however, they present themselves as an 'Austrian breed' (*ratha austriaca*) or 'more Austrian than Italian'. The dialectal term *todésc* may designate inhabitants of the German-speaking countries, but in some cases it is also attached to the people of Trentino in relation to the rest of Italy, and memories of the Great War show this very clearly (Stacul 1998, p. 104). Identifying oneself as 'Austrian' refers to what is perceived as a similarity in terms of 'culture' and values. A recent sociological survey, for instance, has revealed that about 40 per cent of the population in Trentino feels more similar to Austrians than to Italians (Gubert 1997, pp. 475–6).

Some of those who temporarily emigrated to Germany or Switzerland in the 1960s to pursue manual jobs know some German, but this does not mean that they can speak the language correctly. Nowadays, German is taught in national secondary and high schools throughout the regional territory. Schoolchildren between 11 and 14 years of age know some basic German not because they have a chance to learn it from their parents, but because it is a compulsory subject at school. If anything, recent experiences of the local people with German are cited as evidence that this is an altogether foreign language. So, for example, some of the Caorians I met vividly remember what happened during a day trip spent in Innsbruck, an Austrian town not far from the Italian border, in the 1970s. The story goes that a man needed to buy Austrian currency, but he did not know how to do it, because he could not speak a word of German. One of his co-villagers volunteered to help him, on the grounds that he considered himself able to communicate in the language. Eventually it turned out that even this person could not speak German: the women at the counter of the bank where they went could not understand a word of what this man was trying to say, and advised him to express himself in Italian instead, which is widely spoken in that town. This story is sometimes cited as evidence that in the village there is little or no familiarity with that language. It is not purely coincidence that in Caoria the statement 'You speak German' (*ti parli todésc*) usually means 'You speak an incomprehensible language', something nobody is able to understand.

The case of Trentino seems at odds with a situation found in most of Western Europe where, as a response to European integration, national or regional languages become markers of identity and are given political expression. In a sense, linguistic identity (in dialect terms) seems very strong at the local level, but not so much at the regional one, where the *lingua franca* is Italian. Although this seems a contradiction, in fact this shifting salience of language casts light on the flexible character of Trentine identity. In saying so I am not denying the significance of language as a marker of identity: language is powerful when available. Rather, the ethnographic information just presented suggests that when language cannot be used to distinguish the region from the state (or the uplands from the lowlands) territory becomes the main focus of attachment.

So, categories such as 'Italian' and 'Austrian' do not necessarily convey ideas of ethnolinguistic identity, at least at the local level. Nowadays it is the malleability of the meaning attached to these categories that makes it easier, for Trentini, to shift their frame of identification from the 'margins' of Italy to a European region, particularly when the legitimacy of the nation-state is challenged. If one can call oneself 'Italian' by going to live in an Italian city, then one can also call oneself 'Austrian' in a changing political situation. While the party spokesmen's emphasis on Europe can convey ideas of multiculturalism at the regional level, at the local level this rhetoric can also be functional to the legitimization of local identities, all the more so on account of the shifting meaning of the above categories.

Minnich (1998) has analysed a very similar situation on the Austro-Italian-Slovene frontier, where the people involved speak a Slovene dialect, are Italian citizens, express affection for a bi-lingual Carinthia, but no loyalty towards the German nation. As the author argues (1998, pp. 264–5), the use of Slovene dialect does not entail self-identification with any entity larger than the village itself. It is the social actors' perception of the dialect '... as a symbol of collective identity [that] makes them truly peripheral to the region's imagined communities'. They are villagers who have conceptually failed to join a nation. This is similar to the perception of Italian in the Vanoi valley, as has been seen.

The situation so far described is also partly reminiscent of that recorded by Heady in the Carnic Alps (1993, p. 257), in the northeast of Italy, where although language (that is Friulian) was a pivotal issue in the political debate, in fact there was no intention, on the part of the people involved, of replacing Italian with Friulian. In other words, the politicians' construction of a regional identity did not go hand in hand with the people's intention of adopting a language alternative to the national one. Heady's case study is very telling: however, while in the social context he has studied there was little or no intention of giving a political expression to linguistic identity, in the case just analysed there was no intention of giving a linguistic expression to political identity. As far as Trentino is concerned, this is hardly surprising: there are so many dialects in the province that choosing one as the Trentine dialect would mean indifference to differences, all the more so in the construction of a 'transnational' regional identity.

What the Trentine case seems to suggest is the existence of a conceptualization of regional identity which combines various elements that do not necessarily include a common language. A shared history with other ethnic groups seems to be as significant to the idea of region as a territorial, rather than linguistic, unit. Emphasis on territory is far from new; what is unusual is the separation between territory and language, whose boundaries are considered coterminous in nationalist (or regionalist) discourse elsewhere in Europe.

The idea of a multicultural European region had considerable appeal, as it enables social actors to be 'local' while at the same time being part of a putative cosmopolitan and politically-stable 'Europe'. Such an idea reconciles both the emphasis on dialects as markers of distinctiveness within the provincial territory, and that of a shared territorial identity with those who live in the same region, but speak a different dialect. It is a combination of two ideas that apparently contradict each other, that of preserving one's own dialect in a 'global' era, and the reliance upon multiculturalism which is mainly the outcome of the appeal that the current concept of 'Europe' has. This is reminiscent of the shift from a French cultural identity to multiculturalism in Quebec, analysed by Lane Bruner (1997), where such a shift is purely strategic for it serves to assert distinctiveness vis-à-vis a larger encompassing administrative unit such as the nation-state.

The example of Trentino suggests that in a situation of political instability the construction of political and regional identities may take place without language playing a pivotal role. A category such as 'Austrian', in turn, becomes negotiable, even at the local level: those who call themselves Austrians may simply mean that they look upon themselves as partaking of an 'Austrian culture', which may evoke ideas of Europeanness at a time when the concept of Europe is particularly powerful. Social actors can turn Tyroleans or Austrians even though they do not speak a word of German. The idea of Europe itself, with its emphasis on multiculturalism, legitimates the existence of languages without granting to any of these a superior status, and it was by claiming a transnational history that political leaders sought to stress specificity.

Clearly, the idea of a European region had considerable impact in Trentino because it placed emphasis on common origins on the grounds that Trentino, South Tyrol and the Austrian Tyrol shared an almost unbroken history for about 800 years; it also achieved its appeal because it stressed the distinctiveness of the region vis-à-vis a nation-state perceived locally as impersonal and intrusive, and because it championed the transnational character of the region which nowadays is central to the definition of Europe. However, I would not do justice to the meaning attached to such an idea if I were to suggest that it was a mere 'invention' of political leaders. Such an idea was not imposed, but it accommodated itself to local-level discourses, given that being of an 'Austrian breed' is not necessarily perceived as tantamount to having an ethnolinguistic identity.

Conclusions

In 1996, the project of the establishment of 'Euregio' was dropped, particularly after Austria withdrew its support, and after the Italian government strongly discouraged the creation of such a region. Perhaps a relevant aspect that the analysis of Trentine regionalism has revealed is the shifting meaning, at the local level, attached to categories that until recently were synonyms of ethnolinguistic identities. It seems arguable that nowadays 'Austrian' does not necessarily identify German speakers, but is a category which can be appropriated, not to say manipulated, to cope with a political change. Appealing to Europe's multicultural character may serve to stress opposition to the idea of cultural homogeneity which is central to the definition of the nation-state; so, within a multicultural context, one language only can hardly be used as a marker of distinction. In this respect Trentine regionalism did not take the form of an ethnolinguistic revival. This can also be interpreted as the result of the ambivalent meaning attached to the current concept of 'Europe' (especially at the local level), which on the one hand stresses regional identities, and on the other multiculturalism and the obsolescence of national boundaries.

The ethnographic information discussed in this chapter suggests that at the beginning of the millennium the ethnolinguistic community may not be a frame of identification in opposition to the nation-state: identities can be created anew as a consequence of 'Europeanization' or 'globalization'; however, language may not be functional to the attainment of such a goal, given the meanings attached, at the local level, to categories that used to be synonyms of ethnolinguistic identities. At the same time, it is not crucial to impose a language in a territorial unit, such as a European region, that aims to present itself as 'transnational'.

Notes

1. This chapter is the result of research conducted in the course of the PhD in Social Anthropology at the University of Cambridge between 1994 and 1998. Research was funded by the European Union, the Accademia Nazionale dei Lincei and the University of Trieste. I am grateful to Patrick Heady and Camille O'Reilly for their comments on an early draft of this work. Ray Abrahams and Susan Drucker-Brown have also helped with suggestions.
2. Its slogan was 'away from Rome, closer to Europe'.
3. It must be noted that it is hard to posit the existence of fixed regional or local identities in Trentino, given that the human landscape is subject to continuous change. Alpine valleys, for instance, are experiencing an almost irreversible process of depopulation, and immigration to the city of Trent from other Italian regions (not to mention the newly-developing countries) is not an entirely new phenomenon.

Bibliography

Alcock, A. *The History of the South Tyrol Question* (London: Michael Joseph, 1970).

Alcock, A. Trentino and South Tyrol. >From Austrian Crownland to European Region, in *Europe and Ethnicity. The First World War and Contemporary Ethnic Conflict*, S. Dunn and T. Fraser (eds) (London: Routledge, 1996).

Anderson, B. *Imagined Communities* (London: Verso, 1991).

Bourdieu, P. *Language and Symbolic Power* (Cambridge: Polity, 1991).

Cole, J. and Wolf, E. *The Hidden Frontier* (New York: Academic Press, 1974).

Coppola, G. Trentino-Alto Adige: una cultura per difendere la qualità della vita, in *Stato dell'Italia*, P. Ginsborg (ed.) (Milan: Il Saggiatore, 1994).

De Witte, B. Cultural Legitimation: Back to the Language Question, in *European Identity and the Search for Legitimation*, S. Garcia (ed.) (London: Pinter, 1993).

Douglas, M. *Purity and Danger* (London: Routledge, 1966).

Edwards, J. *Language, Society and Identity* (Oxford: Blackwell, 1985).

Friedman, J. The Past in the Future: History and the Politics of Identity, *American Anthropologist* 94 (4) (1992), 837–59.

Friedman, J. *Cultural Identity and Global Process* (London: Sage, 1994).

Gellner, E. *Nations and Nationalism* (Oxford: Blackwell, 1983).

Gubert, R. *Specificità Culturale di una Regione Alpina nel Contesto Europeo; Indagine Sociologica sui Valori dei Trentini* (Milan: Angeli, 1997).

Harvie, C. *The Rise of Regional Europe* (London: Routledge, 1994).

Heady, P. Lingua e identità in Carnia, *S.M. Annali di San Michele* 6 (1993), 257–66.

Heady, P. *The Hard People: Rivalry, Sympathy and Social Structure in an Alpine Valley* (Amsterdam: Harwood Academic, 1999).

Hobsbawm, E. *Nations and Nationalism since 1780* (Cambridge: University Press, 1990).

Hobsbawm, E. Ethnicity and Nationalism in Europe Today, *Anthropology Today* 8 (1) (1992), 3–8.

Judt, T. *A Grand Illusion? An Essay on Europe* (Harmondsworth: Penguin, 1997).

Kedourie, E. *Nationalism* (London: Hutchinson, 1961).

Lane Bruner, M. From Ethnic Nationalism to Strategic Multiculturalism: Shifting Strategies of Remembrance in the Québécois Secessionist Movement, *The Public* 4 (3) (1997), 41–57.

Levy, M. *Governance and Grievance: Habsburg Policy and Italian Tyrol in the Eighteenth Century* (West Lafayette: Purdue University Press, 1988).

Luverà, B. *Oltre il confine. Euregio e conflitto etnico: tra regionalismo europeo e nuovi nazionalismi in Trentino-Alto Adige* (Bologna: Il Mulino, 1996).

Macdonald, S. *Reimagining Culture: Histories, Identities and the Gaelic Renaissance* (Oxford: Berg, 1997).

McDonald, M. *We are not French! Language, Culture and Identity in Brittany* (London: Routledge, 1989).

Miller, D. *On Nationality* (Oxford: University Press, 1995).

Minnich, R. *Homesteaders and Citizens: Collective Identity Formation on the Austro-Italian-Slovene Frontier* (Bergen: Norse, 1998).

O'Reilly, C. The Irish Language as Symbol: Visual Representations of Language in Northern Ireland, in *Symbols in Northern Ireland*, A. Buckley (ed.) (Belfast: The Institute of Irish Studies, 1998).

Poppi, C. The Contention of Tradition: Legitimacy, Culture and Ethnicity in Southern Tyrol, in *Per Frumenzio Ghetta* (Trent: Biblioteca Comunale, 1991).

Renan, E. 'Qu'est ce qu'une nation?', in *Oeuvres complètes de Ernest Renan* (Paris: Calmanm-Lévy, 1947 [1882]).

Sahlins, P. *Boundaries: the Making of France and Spain in the Pyrenees* (Berkeley: University of California Press, 1989).

Sanguanini, B. *Fare cultura. Attori e processi della modernizzazione culturale: il Trentino* (Milan: Angeli, 1992).

Shore, C. and Black, A. Citizens' Europe and the Construction of European Identity, in *The Anthropology of Europe*, V. Goddard *et al.* (eds) (Oxford: Berg, 1994).

Smith, A.D. *The Ethnic Origins of Nations* (Oxford: Blackwell, 1986).

Smith, A.D. *Nations and Nationalism in a Global Era* (Cambridge: Polity, 1996).

Stacul, J. *Between Public and Private: Localism and Local Identity in an Italian Alpine Valley* (Unpublished PhD thesis, University of Cambridge, 1998).

Strassoldo, R. Ethnic Regionalism versus the State: the Case of Italy's Northern Leagues, in *Borders, Nations and States*, L. O'Dowd and T. Wilson (eds) (Aldershot: Avebury, 1996).

Wilson, T. Sovereignty, Identity and Border: Political Anthropology and European Integration, in *Borders, Nations and States*, L. O'Dowd and T. Wilson (eds) (Aldershot: Avebury, 1996).

8
'Old' and 'New' Lesser-Used Languages of Europe: Common Cause?[1]

Tom Cheesman

> If English is now seen to be an 'Indian language' of a sort, why can't Bengali be seen to be a European language of a sort, too?
>
> Ketaki Kushari Dyson (1998)[2]

> Wash your mouth out!
> Primary school teacher in Swansea, Wales, to a pupil speaking Bengali
>
> (reported 1999)

> It's important to be part of Europe. Like, I'm German and European but I won't forget my cultural heritage or mother tongue.
>
> Late-teens South Asian male participant in a *mela* in Düsseldorf, on *Euro Zindagi* ('Euro Life'), Zee TV-Europe
>
> (August 1998)

Europe's non-European and non-white migrants

There is widespread concern in Europe about resurgent nationalisms taking 'cultural-racist' forms in response both to immigration, and to aspects of globalization including efforts to create a common, supra-national European civic culture (Blommaert and Verschueren 1998; Rex 1996). The politics of these developments are highly complex, and mobilizations around lesser-used languages are inescapably involved in them. This chapter raises questions about the relationship between 'new' and 'old' lesser-used languages in the policy of the European Union and member states. The EU context is succinctly analysed by John Rex (1996). The following citation must be read in the context of some 20 million 'non-European' or 'non-white' migrants and their children (and grandchildren, and great-grandchildren) living in the EU today, and some 13 million Moslems of various ethnicities, all of whom throw Europe's conventional self-image into question:

> There is discussion in the European Union today of the possibility of a European identity transcending the identity of nation states. This immediately faces the problem of the resistance arising from the complex nationalisms of member states. It therefore seeks to define itself through a contrast with extra-European entities and to emphasize the elements which the European states have in common. Most often this means differentiating Europeans in terms of their colour and religion. The Union is felt to consist of White Christian nations. This is, however, at odds with any definition which the member states might develop of themselves as multicultural. The position of the ['extra-European' – TC] minorities of the member states is therefore dealt with as a residual problem. Non-white and non-Christian minorities who suffer disadvantage because of their race, colour or religion [or language – TC] have been grouped together with *gastarbeiters*, even though they are politically full citizens, in an organization called the Migrant Forum. All that such a body can do is to unite all these minorities outside the main political framework and to attribute to them a separate identity. The minorities may, it is true, use such a forum to negotiate more effectively with their own nation states, but, if there were a European citizenship and identity, they would not be part of it. The problems here are far from being resolved, and for the moment the European Union will be a union of traditional nation states, all much affected by the ideology of nationalism, but not allowing for the resolution of their problems in dealing with ['extra-European' – TC] ethnic minorities. It is likely indeed to undermine any policies which these nation states might develop, seeking instead to deal itself with migrant minorities in a direct, although residual, way, while also, through its regional policies, offering direct benefits to subnational groups of an autochthonous kind. These contradictory tendencies are likely to mean that it will deal effectively neither with the problem of uniting the nation states nor with the problem of integrating the minorities. (Rex 1996, paragraph 6.1)

Among the 'direct benefits to subnational groups of an autochthonous kind' which are alluded to here, are an increasing variety of measures supporting 'regional and minority languages'. The major supra-national blueprint for language diversity policies which benefit subnational (or would-be national) cultural and linguistic populations, is the *European Charter for Regional or Minority Languages* (Council of Europe 1992). This provides the basis for the implementation of minority language rights in EU states (and some others): rights which are of course contested in many ways in different places, but which nevertheless seem to be generally regarded as a progressive achievement on the road towards cultivating 'diversity'.

The language of the citizen *vis-à-vis* the language of the migrant

Article 1a of the *European Charter* expressly excludes 'languages of migrants'.[3] The rationale for this, in official commentaries, is that only those languages which are spoken by *citizens* or *nationals* of signatory states are appropriately protected by those states: 'Signatory states must choose which languages are to be ... protected. The only conditions ... are that the language *be spoken by the nationals* of a signatory state, and that they belong to a numerically minority group. Official languages, dialects of official languages, and *the languages of migrants are therefore excluded from the outset*' (Council for Cultural Cooperation 1997, p. 35, emphasis added).

This exclusive definition immediately raises questions about disparities between the rights granted to citizens versus non-citizens or 'denizens' (Hammar 1983). It is increasingly true that, whatever the formal citizenship regime may be, in western liberal democracies migrants (unless 'illegal') are generally viewed as being entitled in principle to enjoy the benefits of citizenship and share at least some of the responsibilities (Soysal 1994). This is the case even though, very often, 'the rhetoric of an egalitarian multiculturalism conceals the existence of a multiculturalism based upon inequality' (Rex 1996, paragraph 4.6). But setting that issue aside for the moment, there is also a problem of fact.

The equation between 'migrants' and 'non-citizens' is highly dubious. Users of 'languages of migrants' are by no means all resident aliens. At least in countries where naturalization is easiest, languages spoken by migrants are spoken by citizens within a few years. And children of immigrants, who are usually bilingual, certainly are full citizens, in states which have some form of *ius soli* citizenship law. This means that their formal exclusion from any particular set of rights – such as language rights – has become morally, if not legally, indefensible. One can also foresee a time when it will become politically untenable – unless, of course, migrants themselves 'voluntarily' abandon their languages in the course of 'adaptation', 'integration' or even 'assimilation' to the 'host society'. This is now a key question for the politics of multiculturalism.

Two versions of multiculturalism are distinguished by Rex (1996). A 'strong version' envisages a radical transformation of societies of immigration, leading to quite new forms of 'post-national' society and culture, as majorities amalgamize with minorities. But despite plentiful evidence of new 'hybrid' formations in popular culture (cuisine, music, literature and other arts), and despite high rates of intermarriage between many groups, this vision has little impact on policy. Above all it remains the case that immigrants (and their descendants) make far more fundamental adjustments to the society they live in, than any society adjusts to them. Though an attractive utopian vision, 'strong multiculturalism' is still just that: a vision.

The 'moderate version' of multiculturalism, on the other hand, corresponds to current liberal policy and practice. In Rex's words, it 'accepts that there are institutions which are essential to the modern nation state which will either be entirely secular or based upon shared values, yet at the same time recognizes that there is value in giving limited recognition, for several generations at least, to lively minority cultures', because these cultures both provide for immigrants a 'psychological and moral home between the family and the state', and enable them to organize to fight for their rights collectively (Rex 1996, paragraph 4.9). As well as the adjective 'limited', the *temporal* qualification is crucial here:

> the moderate case for multiculturalism (…) envisages the maintenance of the minority culture (…), not as a matter of permanence, but as referring to a period of three or four generations. After that, what will remain is symbolic ethnicity and the maintenance of a symbolic heritage through festivals and similar occasions. Such symbolic ethnicity is easily accommodated and would generally be regarded as enriching a culture. This does not mean however, that, in the first three or four generations, the recognition of minority cultures should be confined to their exotica, and it does happen that those who are not prepared to deal with the real problems of immigrant minorities do tend to divert attention simply to these exotica. There is in many countries and amongst conservative indigenous groups an avoidance of the tougher areas of negotiation in favour of symbolic ethnic receptions and tea parties. (Rex 1996, paragraph 4.13)

Language, of course, is often viewed, by a majority which does not speak it, as a component of 'exotica'; but it can also be one of those 'tougher areas of negotiation'. I want to suggest that serious negotiations ought to begin on this subject. This is because we cannot assume that the presence in Europe of millions of speakers of Arabic, Bengali, Chinese and so on really is a temporary state of affairs. Motivations for maintaining or – in later generations – re-acquiring extra-European languages are increasing rapidly, and there is much anecdotal evidence available to show that at least some fractions of some communities are strongly cultivating bilingualisms and biliteracies, though as yet little systematic research seems to have been done in this area.

Europe's 'new' minority languages

Languages 'new to Europe'[4] – new, that is, in the past half century or so, mostly – are used by communities varying from a few thousand perhaps, to millions of individuals, often dispersed over several nation-states. The 'new' minority languages of the Europe Union today include very 'big' languages in global demographic and/or economic terms (Arabic, Chinese, Hindi/Urdu, Malay, Russian); national languages of states with varying positions in the world political and economic system (Bengali, Japanese, Korean, Somali, Turkish, etc); and 'local languages … with varying degrees of official recognition' (Graddol 1997, p. 59), including languages which lack an official 'motherland', as they are not state languages anywhere (for example, Kurdish). Even in the case of official state languages, the state in question may be in no position to defend language rights effectively even at home, let alone in the diaspora (this is the case with many Asian and African languages from economically and politically weaker regions).

So, on the one hand, we have the marginalized 'indigenous', 'autochthonous', 'aboriginal' languages which are recognized and increasingly protected and promoted in the EU: languages which have an ancient history in a specific and (in most cases) single territorial base in Europe, and some of which are at risk of extinction. Welsh would be my paradigmatic, UK example. On the other hand, we have marginalized 'immigrant', 'allochthonous' or 'diaspora' languages which are relatively new to Europe. In most but not all cases these have a 'motherland' nation-state outside Europe, and they include languages at no appreciable risk of extinction: thus Bengali or Bangla is now Wales's third language (with most Welsh Bangladeshis speaking the Sylheti dialect), as Turkish is Germany's second language. The cultural political issues and policy options involved are in each such case different. Rather than issues of absolute, global cultural survival, it is local cultural recognition (Taylor 1994) which is most urgently at stake for most migrant communities in Europe. But though different, these issues are far from easy to separate. And the question certainly must be raised: can and should the eurocentric cultural exclusion which is formally enshrined in the 1992 *European Charter* be maintained in the future development of European language diversity policy?

The languages which are covered by the 1992 *European Charter*, which feature for example on the maps published by the European Bureau for Lesser Used Languages, and which are documented by the Mercator projects funded by the European Commission's Ariane programme,[5] hardly form a coherent group. They vary enormously in terms of civic, legal, educational, sociolinguistic, sociocultural and geopolitical position and status; levels of 'endangeredness' due to language shift, and of stigmatization by dominant neighbours; numbers of speakers, and their proportionality, in different territories and localities, with speakers of other languages; and so on. These factors vary so widely that it becomes hard to see just how a line can logically be drawn which excludes the languages of migrants and post-migrant generations: unless by reference to a map of Europe's historical multilingualism which is, quite simply, out of date. It corresponds to the geolinguistics of this region circa 1950.

Not only regional stateless languages are included in the terms of the *European Charter* – Breton, Catalan, Sorbic or Welsh, for example – but also state languages as used by longstanding extraterritorial communities in neighbouring states: Danish, German, Finnish, Slovenian, and so on. It is therefore clear that absolute cultural survival, that is, rescue from threatened extinction, is not in fact the primary issue for legislators: rather, it is the recognition and maintenance of 'diversity', where this concept seems to be inextricably coupled with the eurocratic principle of (subnational) regional cultural autonomy through the devolution of cultural political power. But 'diversity' is also crucially limited by the qualifying measure of ancient territorial continuity.

Romani and Yiddish are acknowledged as exceptions to the rule that a protected language must possess a single, specific territorial base (even if it must be added that measures in support of Romani lag very far behind those adopted in support of the historic languages of Catalonia or Wales; while it is simply too late to protect Yiddish in Europe). So what remains to provide the definitional basis for the regime of cultural protection and targeted development under the *European Charter*? Just one thing: ancient European ancestry, or what might be dubbed the principle of autochthony. The principle behind this legislation is in other words precisely analogous to forms of citizenship law based solely on *ius sanguinis*, which treat the descendants of immigrants as 'foreigners' even unto the nth generation, and which are, rightly, under massive political and moral pressure.

Arabic (classical and national Arabics), Bengali, Chinese (Mandarin, Cantonese, and others), Hindi and Urdu, and many, many other languages which are chiefly used outside geographical or political Europe, and which do not feature at all in projects legitimated by the *European Charter*, are *de facto* important languages of Europe now. They are languages of transnational *and* local communities with increasingly rich *European* cultural heritages: press and other media production, literature, performance and other arts, cultural, educational and other institutions.[6]

'Old' and 'new' cultural minorities

In short, global migration has turned the notion of autochthony into a politically and morally suspect notion: one which places a privileged symbolic value on certain imagined communities and heritages, while others remain unacknowledged, invisible, inaudible. It is the concept of autochthony that underlies the Herderian model of the ethnolinguistically distinctive and territorially anchored *Volk* or *Volksgemeinschaft*. This corresponds to modern 'common-sense' understandings of 'national identity', which define anomalous groups, including both 'old' and 'new' cultural minorities, as 'other', and so marginalize and disadvantage them. But most 'old' minorities can advance their interests by mimicking nationalism on a smaller scale, and claiming regional autonomy in one form or another.[7] New minorities can not. Like Romani speakers, they cannot lay claim to a patch of territory as their own.

Consider, for example, Turkish: the official language of a state on the margins of geopolitical Europe as it is currently configured, a state seeking EU membership, even if it has barely made the shortlist of applicants, and perhaps may never join. The Turkish language features on EBLUL's maps and in Mercator Media's website, in view of its use by an ancient community in Greek Thrace.[8] But as well as the 120 000 members of this particular community (and as well as similar Turkish communities of ancient ancestry in non-EU European countries such as Bulgaria), upwards of 3 million Turkish speakers reside in EU-

Europe. Approximately one third of them were born in the EU, albeit in many cases they are not (yet) EU citizens.[9] (It must also be added that among them are in fact many – often bi/multilingual – speakers of languages which have minority status within Turkey, some of them severely restricted by law there.) Turkish bilingual people – also using the languages of the countries of settlement – are creating culturally specific media and education infrastructures in Germany, the Netherlands, the UK and other countries, but with extremely limited state or EU support, and without any possibility of recourse to legally enforceable claims to entitlement. The contrast with the situation of 'autochthonous' languages is glaring.

Many young people of Turkish parentage or grandparentage, the third generation now living in Western Europe since the mass labour migrations of the 1960s, may have little Turkish; some may not even want to learn Turkish, or not *now*. But others do maintain the language and/or wish they had much better and more varied opportunities to do so. Lack of public recognition of this desire (as also of the desire, in some members of this very fragmented 'community', to use Arabic as the language of Islam, and/or to use one of the many minoritized languages of Turkey), contributes to alienation from the 'host' society and culture even among those who do not personally share such desires, or do not do so at this stage in their lives. And there is every likelihood that such desires will become more rather than less common in the future.

Europe's linguistic diversity is set to increase. New diaspora language communities are being replenished and will carry on being replenished by new migration, often associated with endogamy. They are and will be increasingly in direct communication with 'home/ancestral countries', as well as with co-diaspora communities worldwide. They are and increasingly will be responsible for bringing forth bilinguals who are actively committed to maintaining them as transnational cultural communities, and not least as linguistic communities.

This flies in the face of the standard sociological model of immigrant integration, which, as we have seen, assumes linguistic assimilation – abandonment of all but a symbolic residue of the ancestral language – taking place over the course of three or four generations. But this model may well not hold true, certainly for some languages and groups, in the future. Instead, bi- and multilingualism are becoming the norm. Four main factors contribute to a new trend towards post-migration language maintenance.

Firstly, globalization of communication facilitates the maintenance of languages in diaspora. The real price of air fares and phone calls has been falling for decades, and plummeted in the 1990s. More and more, dispersed linguistic communities – or at least dominant, professional and mobile fractions of them – are bound together by transnational travel and trade, telecommunications, satellite/cable television and other media, including email and Internet services. The latter include the emergent commercial development of print-on-demand and distributed printing, enabling publications to be distributed globally via the Internet and printed in small runs for local niche markets; as well as Internet radio services, which deliver local media to global audiences. This enables (for instance) the London-based journalist John Naughton to listen to the RTE daily news in order to keep up his Irish, wherever he is in the world (Naughton 1999). In a similar way, a colleague remarked to me recently that: 'It feels very different being Welsh since the Internet'.[10] Assorted media, educational and cultural initiatives exploiting ICT are now connecting Welsh speakers in Wales, in England and around the world, from Patagonia to Norway to Japan, in quite unprecedented ways, creating a global Welsh-language public sphere. What holds for an 'old' marginalized European language, and its quite small global diaspora, holds no less for many 'new', marginalized, *de facto* European languages. While transnational networking encourages the spread of English, it also encourages the dispersed development of other languages. The most important new European languages are also languages of access to majorities in other countries. This brings us to the second factor.

Secondly, economic globalization means that so-called 'heritage bilinguals' have real advantages in the global economy. They are equipped to access multiple markets, relying on networks sustained by kinship and co-ethnic trust. This means growing incentives for individuals to cultivate any languages they can call their own, and not only globally or regionally dominant languages, but others besides. Maintenance and revival of familial, community and ancestral languages can be meant as a symbolic gesture affirming 'hybrid' and 'resistant' minoritarian identities. But there are also wholly objective, economic motives. Their speciality languages enable people to access niche markets, both in 'ancestral countries' or 'back home', as well as throughout the transnational linguistic community. The world of global 'tribes' portrayed by Joel Kotkin (1994), in which (certain kinds of) Britons, Jews, Armenians, Chinese, Indians and other transnational groups are (or were) the motor of economic development everywhere they settle, is an increasingly complex reality – increasingly complex, because little 'tribes' as well as big ones are now able to use the same strategies, and find it easier to do so for the technological and economic reasons just outlined. Economic expansion or liberalization in the ancestral country (as an 'emergent market') is a major incentive here, but diaspora languages can be economically useful even in the absence of such development, when a network of expatriate communities offers opportunities in other places.

Thirdly, general educational, psychological and social benefits can be conferred by bilingual backgrounds, when supported by formal education encouraging balanced bilingualism. This is now very widely recognized. So too are the serious disadvantages which are often suffered when one's home or community language is not supported in education. As a result, wherever there are significant numbers of users of non-official or unrecognized languages, pressures for their maintenance and development, at least in the educational sphere, are certain to mount. They will probably also tend to move beyond the purely educational sphere, into broader spheres of media and civil society. Here the struggles by and on behalf of indigenous territorial minorities can impact on the consciousness and aspirations of migrant groups in as yet uncharted ways. The global rise of the politics of identity and more particularly of language rights as a political issue, symbolized by UNESCO's institution of an International Mother Language Day (first celebrated on 21 February 2000),[11] reinforces this trend.

Fourthly, state policymakers in some western countries are beginning to view minority language skills as a valuable economic resource. A report by the London Research Centre in 1999 stressed the value of language diversity in attracting jobs to the city, such as the Air France call centre which relocated recently to London from Paris, to take advantage of the pool of language expertise.[12] Bilingualism lobbyists have shifted ground from purely educationalist and even rights-based arguments towards arguments from economic rationality. Thus, in the USA, the (national) Centre for Applied Linguistics and the National Foreign Language Centre have launched a Heritage Language Initiative in order to 'help the U.S. education system recognize and develop the heritage language resources of this country as part of a larger effort to educate citizens who can function professionally in English and other languages'.[13] A growing body of work on 'home languages' (Soto *et al.* 1999), 'heritage languages' (Brecht and Ingold 1998) and 'ethnic literacy' (Brecht and Ingold 1998; Elmallah and Gezi 1996) – though all these terms are intrinsically problematic as they still imply a monolingual norm and associate only English with modernity[14] – exhibits not just a concern with the ethics of social distinction and the politics of identity and recognition, and not just a concern with the need for diverse knowledges and wisdoms in social development. There is increasingly a pragmatic concern about access to knowledges and markets beyond the reach of English, making professionalized language diversity a valuable resource for all social-political scales from local to national to international.

Cultural and linguistic change?

To what extent and just how such factors will transform the processes of cultural and linguistic change undergone by 'other-language-speaking' migrants, it is still too soon to say. It remains the case that 'the problems of minorities, and especially of recent immigrants, are not in the first place linguistic ones but rather serious economic ones', and that 'mastering the dominant languages offers more advantages' *locally* 'than competence in minority languages' (Pasch 1999, p. 101). But, increasingly, new Europeans are not the stereotypical down-trodden labour migrants. Rather, they are economically successful and transnationally mobile professionals, who count multilingualism among their skills.

Many commentators still doubt that the longstanding pattern of language obsolescence is changing or will change. One who thinks it is changing is the Canadian/Quebecker multiculturalist philosopher, Charles Taylor, probably the most influential theorist of the politics of recognition (Taylor 1994). He is a supporter of Quebec's Bill 101, which provides resources and incentives for immigrants to Quebec to learn French rather than English as a public language. He envisages the fostering of *bilingual* diversity leading to *multilingual* diversity, with migrant communities maintaining distinct cultures, including languages. Certainly his views do not go unchallenged (Lamey 1999). It is likely that worldwide, migrants are in the forefront of learning languages for mobility and opportunity – English for business and professional purposes above all. It would seem to follow that erosion or loss of ancestral languages will remain the norm, perhaps particularly in non-English-speaking countries (trilingualism being even more demanding than bilingualism). However, it is extremely risky to generalize across either migrant or regional communities, and about different groups within such communities. People and groups adopt different strategies at different moments. But the example of Hispanics in the USA already shows that, where geographical, demographic and social conditions are right, language maintenance is a very real option

– even in the face of monolingual state policies, or grudgingly and minimally multilingual policies.

Taylor's 'belief that immigrant cultures can perpetuate themselves within a host democracy' is regarded even by one of his admirers, Ray Conlogue, in a letter defending him against Lamey's critique, as an implausible 'adventure into the far reaches of liberal thought from which Taylor may or may not return alive, intellectually speaking' (Conlogue 1999). Lamey (1999) alleged that Bill 101 discriminates against all languages except French. Writing as a supporter of Taylor's liberal multiculturalism and Bill 101, Conlogue holds to the idea that 'immigrants do not wish to perpetuate' their own languages: 'Instead, they long to integrate themselves and their children into the culture of the new country'. But this standard generalization needs to be modified: where possible, immigrants and children of immigrants prefer bilingualism, certainly where issues of race and religion effectively preclude full assimilation. On the same page, another supporter of Taylor and of Bill 101, Mark Abley, points out proudly that 'in Montreal, more than any other Canadian city, young people from cultural minorities still speak the languages of their ancestors. The decision to speak or abandon a language is not just a matter of law but of social psychology' (Abley 1999). In Quebec, it seems, aboriginal languages thrive (more than elsewhere in North America, at least) and so do the diverse languages of what might be called 'newcomers'. The implication is that Quebeckers' sensitivity to issues of language and identity, a consciousness produced primarily by the tensions between anglophonia and francophonie, and secondarily between this dominant pair and the languages of First Nations and of other-language migrants, results in an active, participatory politics of recognition of the full range of multi-bilingualisms. The national public languages are used alongside 'subnational community' languages.

Yet none of the parties in this particular public debate seems to appreciate that 'subnational community' languages are also often – increasingly often – 'transnational community' languages. They are not merely significant to local communities, nor even just used in contacts between these communities and ancestral countries. Conlogue believes that Taylor's position and the aims of Bill 101 can be generalized, but only to 'cover situations where a minority language has a territorial base'. Abley suggests that 'extra-territorial' languages are also an important part of the equation: maintenance of such languages is a sign of engagement in the development of local cultural diversity and a politics of inclusion of the 'other'. What needs to be added here is that this is often also a sign of engagement in transnational cultures other than (and as well as) the anglophone or the francophone. As Karim H. Karim points out, again from a Canadian perspective, 'ethnic community media' are in fact, increasingly, global media: not only Spanish but Chinese, Hindi, Arabic, as well as many other, less massively populous language cultures, are transnationally networked in media production and reception across the continents (Karim 1999).

Such North American debates are followed with great interest in Europe. But fears about cultural fragmentation, conflict and persecution are yet more vivid here. The 'other languages' of minorities, old or new, have tended to be refused recognition because, in the words of Hans Ulrich Gumbrecht:

> the flip side of emphasising cultural particularity (...) is the danger of affirming nationalisms and regionalisms, with all the feelings of superiority and the spirit of resentment that such attitudes can imply. There is a price to be paid (...). The establishment of linguistic boundaries is one such consequence, and we know that their reappearance is not always simply a return to an original situation of difference that was repressed by a centralising power. Should we forbid ourselves to ask the question of how many lives the Yugoslavian government of the Tito era would have saved by allowing for less cultural and linguistic diversity? (Gumbrecht 1997, p. 253)

The 'Balkan nightmare' which haunts the European Union certainly has complex linguistic dimensions. They are implied by the infamous Serb slogan, a summation of vulgar and deadly Herderianism: 'One country, one language, one religion, one alphabet' (cited in Ganahl 1998, p. 360). They are instanced, perhaps, by the fate of a United Nations international staff member, beaten and killed on the main street of Pristina in October 1999, apparently for mistakenly replying in Serbian to someone who asked the time. But it is far from clear that language is a causative factor in any of the conflicts, rather than one axis of difference which is mobilized by politicians who seek advantage from conflict. Nor is it clear that enforced assimilation to any imposed cultural and linguistic norm would lead to preferable outcomes, even if it were feasible (or in the Yugoslav case, if it had been). Rather, it might be that policies designed to disentangle identity and diversity from territory, re-mapping diversities onto territories in more flexible ways, could help prevent the hardening of boundaries.

There are alternatives to the strictly exclusive concept of 'linguistic minorities' which is enshrined in the *European Charter* of 1992. For example, the text of the *Universal Declaration of Linguistic Rights* (CIEMEN 1996) (also known as the 'Barcelona Declaration'), makes a point of including language groups which lack the 'territorial antecedents' of indigenous or autochthonous communities. The *Universal Declaration* 'also considers as a language group any group of persons sharing the same language which is established in the territorial space of another language community but which does not possess historical antecedents equivalent to those of that community. Examples of such groups are *immigrants, refugees, deported persons and diasporas*' (Article 1.5, emphasis added).[15] The policy implications of this broader understanding of linguistic rights demand some very careful consideration, which may soon be forced on states, whether by supranational organizations from above, or by social movements from below.

Conclusions

It can be argued that language rights should properly be viewed as 'culture-language-context-specific rights' ('emic rights'), and that to consider them from a universal rights perspective 'overstates issues and masks rights *to* as also being rights *against*' (Paulston 1997, p. 82). But for good or for ill, notions of language rights as universal are spreading, and after all, legislation does exist (and can be reformed). If legislation is not based on presumptive universal rights, it develops categories of 'minority', where different definitions of 'minority' are intrinsically political decisions.

One notion of 'linguistic minority' might set any given language in relation to the global dominant language. Over 50 per cent of published translations in the world (and rising) are translations from English.[16] This traffic is mostly one-way: under 3 per cent of world publications in English are translations from other languages.[17] There are a handful of world-regional interlinguas – Arabic, Chinese, Hindi/Urdu, Spanish – but English is the major language of interregional communication and trade: *the* 'global language' (Crystal 1997; Graddol 1997). In an important sense, then, all languages other than English are becoming, in relation to English, 'minoritized' languages. Welsh (with 250 thousand speakers) is only a degree less minoritized than German (with about 100 million). Those languages that survive globalization at all are tending to become languages of identity and heritage, functioning in relatively restricted (even if socially huge) spheres, while English is the planetary *lingua franca* of groups with technical, economic, and political power-knowledge. The EU may be becoming a kind of multilingual empire, but it is only a province in the virtual, global empire of anglophonia.

In the face of this many-faceted trend, one facet of which is the hastening extinction of the majority of natural languages around the world, experts on 'world Englishes' and advisors to the global ELT industry see the ethical and political dimensions of language policy becoming ever more important, and even (for them) scary. Thus, Graddol paints a nightmare scenario in which the global spread of English becomes associated worldwide with 'industrialisation, the destruction of cultures, infringement of basic human rights, global cultural imperialism and widening social inequality', provoking some kind of catastrophic reversal of English's recent fortunes (Graddol 1997, pp. 62–3). It is partly against this backdrop that the minority language protection policies adopted in Europe (the EU, constituent states and applicant states) are now in urgent need of rethinking: they need to address global concerns about cultural injustice.

At present the concepts on which Europe's language diversity policy is premised are those of ancient territorial continuity and 'indigenous' heritage conservation. Without jettisoning these concerns entirely, policy should instead be governed by concepts of global cultural diversity and transnational network-building. Such a policy shift would recognize two major contemporary cultural shifts: first, towards multiple and hybrid identities, as a consequence of accelerated 'time–space compression', in other words cheaper and faster traffic in goods, people and signs within a trans-global 'cosmopolis'; and second, from the pre-eminence of 'one-to-many' media such as print and broadcasting, which tend to maintain the hegemony of standardized nation-state languages, to 'many-to-many' media such as telephony and the Internet, which are infinitely more favourable to diversity. The sociolinguistic impact of mobile phones remains to be seen, and there seems to be little speculation. Not so with the Internet, which is said to amount to 'a radically new medium both for the reinforcement of minority and immigrant languages and for the development and spread of planned languages' (Fettes 1997, n.p., citing Nunberg 1996, n.p.). Planned languages will surely remain utopian. But in real places where real people speak (and read and write), that adjectival couple 'minority and immigrant' is becoming ever more pertinent.

A survey in London in 1989 counted 160 languages in regular use; in 1993, it was estimated that 275 languages were regularly spoken in the capital; and in 1999, a total closer to 300 is estimated. The differences may have less to do with actual increases in diversity than with more refined survey techniques, and of course the largely political distinction between languages and dialects plays a role. But there are now said to be 33 so-called 'ethnic' communities in London of over 10 000 people (this is based on a count of people born in countries outside England), and a good many of these are not ancestrally anglophone. Perhaps the most dramatic figure: a language other than English is spoken in about 30 per cent of London homes.[18]

Of course London is far from typical. It can even boast that it is the most multilingual city in the world, with the possible exception of New York. Nevertheless, in the UK, this language diversity is not confined to the capital. A recent survey in Sheffield, Yorkshire, counted 189 languages in use in that city.[19] And even far less metropolitan regions and towns are now surprisingly diverse. Without attempting a proper sociolinguistic survey, over 40 'communities' are identified by the Race Equality Council in the Swansea Bay district of South Wales, a region which has seen relatively little extra-European immigration. Most of these communities are not ancestrally anglophone (and nor are they Welsh-speaking). But they are striking roots in Wales. Local authorities and voluntary groups endeavour to support immigrants' acquisition of English (and Welsh), on minimal resources. Little or nothing is on offer to support the maintenance of their own first languages.

So far, there are few signs that people with an investment in autochthonous language rights in Europe are seriously addressing the question of the new European languages. Concluding his survey of the development of bilingual Wales, from his vantage point in Canada, Colin H. Williams (1995) points to two areas in need of further research: the Welsh diasporas, and international comparative perspectives. Re-considering 'the Welsh in the world' is now evidently closely connected with a turn away from comparisons only with other Celts or with places such as Friesland, Euskadi and Friuli, for:

> we are constraining ourselves if we only make common cause and comparisons with lesser-used language regions, rather than with smaller states such as Norway and Denmark, and overseas proto-states such as Quebec. (...) Today we are in danger of compounding this narrow vision of a bicultural Wales by emphasising questions

of marginality, peripherality and relative deprivation. I do not believe this is the lasting reality of Wales. European, Japanese and American inward investment suggests otherwise. (Williams 1995, pp. 75–6)

What this reveals, once again, is the way that progressive language agendas are seduced by the conjuncture of European devolution and globalization. Many in Wales remain desperately deprived, though language may have nothing whatever to do with it: more monoglot English speakers are living in poverty than Welsh speakers or Sylheti or Arabic or Somali speakers. But if bilingualism is to be cultivated in Wales, it can no longer credibly be only Welsh–English bilingualism. The ethical and political impetus which has given credibility to the language movement here has surely gone, as soon as questions of marginalization are written out of the picture; and questions of marginalization cannot remain exclusive to autochthonous communities in Wales any more than elsewhere in the rich North and West of the world.

A European Union which legislates and passes budgets to protect its aboriginal languages, while still discriminating against all the languages of relative newcomers, must seem simply unjust, and the premises of its policy untenable. New European languages are commonly used by people who do not conform to outdated prejudices as to what a European is supposed to *look* like, as well as sound like. The challenging implications of such observations for cultural and language policy are becoming widely recognized. It is symptomatic and encouraging that the Arts Council of England has announced a prioritization of 'internal translation', meaning translation between the diverse languages actually in use in the UK, with the specific aim of serving transnational communities.[20] But this is little more than a token gesture (though token gestures too are important).[21] And as yet, it seems that debates in Europe are mostly conducted quite separately on 'old' and 'new' language diversities, because the policy and research infrastructures have evolved quite separately.

Those campaigning for the recognition, protection, promotion and sustained development of the diverse languages of *old* Europe would strengthen their moral and political position enormously by seeking alliances with the full range of minoritized language communities of the Europe we now really inhabit, in order to develop collaborative educational, cultural and media initiatives. This could help build a future Europe more open to the cultures of the rest of the world as well as to its internal creative diversity; a Europe more fully engaged in transnational social development with international partners both inside and beyond the region.

Notes

1. This paper is based on work carried out for the Axial Writing Project in the Transnational Communities Research Programme, funded by the Economic and Social Research Council (UK), award L214252030. Earlier versions were presented at the Workshop on Media in Multilingual and Multicultural Settings, sponsored by the ESRC and the Council of Europe (Klagenfurt, 11–14 Nov. 1999), and the Mosaic International Conference on the Promotion of Literature Across Borders, at the Mercator Media Centre for Minority Languages of the European Union (Aberystwyth, 12–14 November 1998).

2. Ketaki Kushari Dyson, 'Notes Towards a Preface', in Dyson, 1998, p. 5. Dyson's literary work is celebrated in the Bengali-speaking world; she has been resident in England for over 30 years, writes diverse genres in both languages, and translates both ways, but prefers Bengali for her novels and plays.

3. Article 1a reads: '"regional or minority languages" means languages that are: (i) *traditionally* used within a given territory of a State by nationals of that State who form a group numerically smaller than the rest of the State's population; and (ii) different from the official language(s) of that State; *it does not include either dialects of the official language(s) of the State or the languages of migrants'* (Council of Europe, 1992, emphasis added). Note that diverse governmental and non-governmental texts on linguistic rights are accessible via UNESCO's MOST Clearing House Linguistic Rights at <http://www.unesco.org/most/ln1.htm>.

4. The term 'new to Europe' is as problematic as any other: Arabic, say, was spoken in 'Europe' as long ago as any modern European language; and is Turkey not (at least partly) 'in Europe'? Yet just as, say, the Black African diaspora presence in Britain can be traced back to Roman times (Fryer 1984), while large Afro-diasporic *communities* are more recently established, so too with languages: the contemporary situation of both real and virtual proximity is new.

5. See the site of the European Bureau for Lesser-Used Languages at <http://www.eblul.org>. Mercator Media (Aberystwyth) is part of a EU network documenting and supporting lesser-used languages, funded under the EC Ariane programme: see <http://www.aber.ac.uk/~merwww>.

6. The 'Axial Writing Project' (see note 1, above) is making an interdisciplinary study of Caribbean, Irish, South Asian and Turkish transnational literary and media cultural production in Britain and Germany, and of relevant national and European cultural policy. See <http://www.transcomm.ox.ac.uk> (links under 'Research') for details.

7. Demands for full national autonomy are receding in Europe behind demands for quasi-national regional autonomy within a supra-national federal system, as instanced by Catalonia (where language is central to the

assertion of a distinctive identity) and Wales (where the language issue is less central because the great majority of citizens and denizens speak no Welsh). Though stopping short of demanding full national sovereignty, particularly in the realms of security and foreign policy, such regions nonetheless aspire to quasi-national status. On Catalonia, see Castells, 1997, 42–50.

8. See <http://www.aber.ac.uk/~merwww/links2.htm#Türkçe>.
9. In Germany alone, there live over two million Turkish passport-holders of diverse ethnicity (and, now, varying levels of competence in Turkish): mostly Turkish mononationals; some Turkish-German binationals. There are relatively few naturalized former Turkish nationals. In late 1998 the new 'Red–Green' government announced major modifications to the citizenship law, to facilitate naturalization and dual citizenship (hitherto only unofficially available), and to confer German citizenship automatically on migrants' grandchildren. Furious resistance from the formerly governing Right (including a populist petition which claimed to have gathered six million signatures against the dual citizenship proposals in a few weeks, and won the state of Hessia for the conservatives for the first time in many decades) led to a watering-down of the proposals, in particular restricting dual citizenship to under-23s: at that age, binationals will have to choose one citizenship. But the principle of *jus soli*, conferring German citizenship on immigrants' children born in Germany (subject to some restrictions), came into effect on 1 January 2000. Naturalization still involves a language test.
10. Robert Rhys, Lecturer in Welsh at University of Wales Swansea: personal communication, July 1999. See also Pamela Petro's reportage (1998), a fascinating exploration of Welsh as a global language; she begins her intercontinental journey by using the Internet to contact Welsh-speaking groups around the world.
11. The proposal came from Bangladesh. See <http://www.mydhaka.com/wml.htm>. The day was marked in Swansea by an afternoon of celebratory events organized by secular activists in the Bengali-speaking community, with Lord Dafydd Elis-Thomas (Presiding Officer of the National Assembly of Wales) as guest of honour. Here was a powerful symbolic representative of 'bilingual' Wales, obliged to confront the continuing discrimination of Bengali – and other new languages of Wales.
12. Cited in *The Independent* (29 March 1999) and *Evening Standard* (30 June 1999).
13. 'Heritage Language Initiative': <http://www.cal.org/public/heritage.htm> (9/15/99).
14. The concept 'heritage language' suggests a second-class status: whereas English is modern, other languages are pre-modern. For some purposes this simply is the case. At an extreme is the insight of 'aboriginal folks, so-called' in Eastern Kimberley region, Australia, 'who use an expression that can be translated into mainstream Australian English as "lost our language", by which they mean that they no longer compute with their cultural idiom. (...) [T]hey do not mean they have forgotten how to speak their language. (...) They mean that they no longer make sense of their lives in terms of their cultural idiom' (Spivak 1998, p. 183).

15. The *Universal Declaration of Linguistic Rights* was drafted by members of International PEN and CIEMEN/Mercator (Barcelona), and co-signed by representatives of about a hundred NGOs. It is en route from UNESCO to the UN. See <http://www.linguistic-declaration.org> and <http://www.partal.com/ciemen/conf/index.html> (with English, Spanish, Catalan and French texts), and <http://www.troc.es/mercator/main-gb.htm> for background information.

16. UNESCO 1998, Tables 19–21 (pp. 441–7). See also Held 1999, Table 7.3, p. 346.

17. Held 1999, Table 7.3, p. 346, shows 4 per cent of UK book publications (1983–85) were translations, but only 0.3 per cent of US book publications.

18. For the 1989 figure see Bourne, 1997, p. 52. Other figures from *The Independent* (29 March 1999) and *Evening Standard* (30 June 1999), citing research at SOAS in 1993, and the London Research Centre in 1999. Compare a figure from the US national census of 1990: 14 per cent of all children aged 5 to 17 (about 6.3 million) were reported as not speaking English at home (Soto, Smrekar, and Nekcovei 1999).

19. Figure supplied by Martin Dutch of Sheffield City Libraries, reporting on the 'Multilingual City' survey and public awareness campaign at the 'Translation and Community' conference (Third ITI International Colloquium on Literary Translation, University of Sheffield, 1–3 Sept 1998).

20. Gary McKeone (Senior Literature Officer, Arts Council of England) speaking at the ITI 'Translation and Community' conference (note 19 above).

21. Australia is pioneering good practice in the field of post-migration language diversity. Initiatives which might be emulated by European states, or indeed supranational European agencies, include the Deakin University Multicultural Writers Project (Gunew 1992), a database of Australian writers of LOTE (languages other than English) or of NESB (non-English-speaking background). The book features over 600 writers (with biographical details and critical appraisals) belonging to 38 national/linguistic groups. An update on CD-ROM has been announced (see also Board of Studies 1999). No comparable signal of the recognition of cultural diversity as language diversity exists to my knowledge anywhere in Europe.

Bibliography

Abley, M. [Letter re: Lamey, 1999], *Times Literary Supplement*, 5029 (August 20, 1999), 15.

Blommaert, J. and Verschueren, J. *Debating Diversity* (London: Routledge, 1998).

Board of Studies New South Wales. *Making Multicultural Australia* (CD-ROM package). Sydney: Board of Studies New South Wales, 1999.

Bourne, J. '"The Grown-Ups Know Best": Language Policy-Making in Britain in the 1990s', *Language Policy: Dominant English, Pluralist Challenges*, W. Eggington and H. Wren (eds) (Amsterdam: John Benjamins, 1997), pp. 49–65.

Brecht, R.D. and Ingold, C.W. 'Tapping a National Resource: Heritage Languages in the United States', *ERIC Digest*, November 1998 <http://www.cal.org/ericcll/digest/brecht01.html>.

Castells, M. *The Power of Identity* (Blackwell: Malden MA and Oxford, 1997).

CIEMEN. *Universal Declaration of Linguistic Rights* 1996 <http://www.linguistic-declaration.org>.

Conlogue, R. [Letter re: Lamey, 1999], *Times Literary Supplement*, 5029 (August 20, 1999), 15.

Council for Cultural Cooperation (CDCC). *Project 'Democracy, Human Rights, Minorities: Educational and Cultural Aspects'. Final Conference, 21–23 May 1997, Strasbourg. Cultural Rights at the Council of Europe (1949–1996).* Report. Strasbourg: CDCC (DECS/SE/DHRM (97) 5), 1997.

Council of Europe. *European Charter for Regional or Minority Languages*, 1992 <http://www.coe.fr/eng/legaltxt/148e.htm>.

Crystal, D. *English as a Global Language* (Cambridge: Cambridge University Press, 1997).

Dyson, K.K. *Night's Sunlight. Translated from the Original Bengali by the Author* (unpublished typescript, Oxford, 1998).

Elmallah, A. and Gezi, K. 'Popular Ethnic Literacy: Participatory Research and Heritage Language Learning of Korean-American College Students', paper at the 40th Annual Meeting of the Comparative and International Education Society, Williamsburg, Virginia, March 6–10, 1996 <http://www.hku.hk/cerc/cies96/4-8.htm>.

Fettes, M. 'Interlinguistics and the Internet', 1997 <www.magi.com/~mfettes/internet.html>.

Fryer, P. *Staying Power: Black People in Britain Since 1504* (London: Pluto, 1984).

Graddol, D. *The Future of English?* The British Council, 1997.

Ganahl, R. 'Lesen, Sprechen, Lernen, Lehren', *Imported: a Reading Seminar*, R. Ganahl (ed.) (New York: Semiotext(e), 1998), pp. 350–64.

Gumbrecht, H.U. 'Epilogue: Untenable Positions', *Streams of Cultural Capital*, D. Palumbo-Lui and H.U. Gumbrecht (eds) (Stanford: Stanford University Press, 1997), pp. 249–62.

Gunew, S. *et al. Bibliography of Australian Multicultural Writers* (Geelong, Victoria: Deakin University Press, 1992).

Hammar, T. *European Immigration Policy: a Comparative Study* (Cambridge: Cambridge University Press, 1983).

Held, D., McGrew, A. Goldblatt, D. and Perraton, J. *Global Transformations: Politics, Economics and Culture* (Cambridge: Polity Press, 1999).

Karim, K.H. 'From Ethnic Media to Global Media: Transnational Communication Networks Among Diasporic Communities', paper prepared for Canadian Heritage, International Comparative Research Group, June 1998, Transnational Communities Programme Working Paper 99-02, 1999 <http://www.transcomm.ox.ac.uk>.

Kotkin, J. *Tribes. How Race, Religion and Ethnicity Determine Success in the New Global Economy* (New York: Random House, 1994).

Lamey, A. 'Francophonia For Ever. The Contradiction in Charles Taylor's "Politics of Recognition"', *Times Literary Supplement*, 5027 (July 23, 1999) 12–15.

Naughton, J. 'This is Where it's @', *The Observer*, 22 August 1999, 'Review', p. 3.

Nunberg, G. 'E-Babel', *Esperantic Studies*, 7, 3–4 (1996): 1–21.

Pasch, H. Review of *Sociolinguistica*, Vol. 9, *European Identity and Language Diversity* (1995), *Word*, 50, 1 (1999): 97–102.

Paulston, C.B. 'Language Policies and Language Rights', *Annual Review of Anthropology*, 26 (1997) 73–85.

Petro, P. *Travels in an Old Tongue: Touring the World Speaking Welsh* (London: Flamingo, 1998).

Rex, J. 'National Identity in the Democratic Multi-Cultural State', *Sociological Research Online*, 1:2 (1996) *http://www.socresonline.org.uk/socresonline/1/2/1.html*.

Soto, L.D., Smrekar, J.L. and Nekcovei, D.L. 'Preserving Home Languages and Cultures in the Classroom: Challenges and Opportunities', *Directions in Language and Education* (National Clearinghouse for Bilingual Education), 13 (Spring 1999) <http://www.ncbe.gwu.edu/ncbepubs/directions/13.htm>.

Soysal, Y.N. *Limits of Citizenship: Migrants and Postnational Membership in Europe* (Chicago: University of Chicago Press, 1994).

Spivak, G.C. 'Lost Our Language – Underneath the Linguistic Map. Interview by R. Ganahl', *Imported: a Reading Seminar*, R. Ganahl (ed.) (New York: Semiotext(e), 1998), pp. 182–92.

Taylor, C. 'The Politics of Recognition', *Multiculturalism: Examining the Politics of Recognition*, A. Gutmann (ed.) (Princeton NJ: Princeton University Press, 1994), pp. 25–74.

UNESCO. *World Culture Report 1998: Culture, Creativity and Markets* (Paris: UNESCO, 1998).

Williams, C.H. 'The Development of Bilingual Wales', *Bilingualism, Education and Identity. Essays in Honour of Jac L. Williams*, B.M. Jones and P.A.S. Ghuman (eds) (Cardiff: University of Wales Press, 1995), pp. 47–78.

Index

174 *Index*